POWER, MONEY & SEX

How Success Almost Ruined My Life

Deion Sanders
with Jim Nelson Black

WORD PUBLISHING
NASHVILLE
A Thomas Nelson Company

Unless otherwise noted, Scripture quotations are from the NEW KING JAMES VERSION. Copyright ©
1979, 1980, 1982, 1992, Thomas Nelson, Inc., Publishers.

Scripture quotations noted KJV are taken from the KING JAMES VERSION.

Scripture quotations noted NIV are taken from the HOLY BIBLE: NEW INTERNATIONAL VERSION®.
Copyright © 1973, 1978, 1984 by International Bible Society. Used by permission of Zondervan
Publishing House. All rights reserved.

ISBN: 0-8499-1499-X

Printed in the United States of America
9 0 1 2 3 4 5 BVG 9 8 7 6 5 4 3

This book is dedicated

To my fathers, Mims Sanders and Will Knight:
Whose lives, combined, gave me the love, attention, and affection that I needed. Because of their dedication and support—whether on the fifty-yard-line or rooting from the parking lot—they will forever serve as my inspiration. Every time I step onto the football field, the baseball diamond, or into the pulpit, I know they're there with me, encouraging and cheering me on, because they are truly my biggest fans.

To my beloved, beautiful children, Deiondra and Deion, Jr.:
Thank you for the hugs and kisses and the countless times we've exchanged the words, "I love you."

To the bleeding men, especially the athletes:
Who are still on the outside looking in, and who have refused so far to enter God's training room to get cared for. You know what I'm sayin'—

CONTENTS

POWER, MONEY, & SEX

ACKNOWLEDGMENTS

There are so many people who are a part of my story and who need to be recognized. I would like to express my gratitude to all of them. First of all, to my family, Connie Knight, Tracy Knight, Hattie Mims, Billy Jones, and Scoodie Moss. And to my spiritual parents, Bishop T. D. Jakes & Serita Jakes.

I also want to express appreciation to Bishops Eddie Long, Noel Jones, Carlton & Gina Pearson, and William James; to Pastors David & Tracy Forbes, Terry & Rene Hornbuckle, Dr. Leroy Thompson, Dr. Mark Hanby, and Kenneth Hagin, Jr.; and to Ministers Mike Barber and Martin Johnson.

I owe a special debt of gratitude to my attorney for life, Eugene Parker, as well as to Jerry Jones, and all my past and present coaches, including Little League Baseball. Thanks to Dave & Helen Capel, and to my teammates past and present, from Pop Warner Football on.

Thanks to my editor, Dr. Jim Nelson Black, who assisted in the writing and preparation of this book; to Mr. and the late Mrs. Dewey; to all the folks at South Dallas Nursing Home: to the faithful saints at Prime Time Tuesdays; and last but not least, to all my homeys who are saying, "I can't believe this brotha forgot me!" I didn't forget you man. God bless you!

FOREWORD

I will always remember learning in school a marketing concept that was referred to as "bait and switch." Bait and switch is a concept of marketing where rather unscrupulous persons use false advertising to entice consumers to come in the store for a particular product and then substitute it with a subordinate product. You can imagine how destructive it is for the consumer to arrive at the store only to find that the product advertised has been substituted with something far different than he expected. This unscrupulous technique is a perfect metaphor of our life experience, as we tend to live in a world that promises everything and delivers very little. Tragically, many of us live our whole lives never noticing that what we dreamed to achieve in life has been substituted with some mere token of accomplishment.

In Deion Sander's newly released book, *Power, Money, and Sex,* he graphically depicts and declares the destructive and disappointing pursuit of these three entities. In and of themselves, they are not detrimental, but when power, money, and sex are misappropriated, the effects are catastrophic. Many men's lives have been altered by the use or abuse of this trinity of danger. If we are to use them appropriately, we need sound counsel. Who else would be better to speak to this generation in regard to the false advertising of these three areas than Mr. PMS would? His nick names, Prime Time and Neon Deion, are descriptive of Deion's acquisition of a fool's gold that turned to dust and slipped through the crevices of a clenched fist, while his angry heart searched desperately for answers that seemed to evade his grasp. Neither power, money, nor sex had produced their advertised happiness. His is a resurrected voice back from the grave of deceit to tell us how he walked the streets of success that led to a near fatal end. He returns not renouncing any of the three but rather warning us of the dangers of idolizing or abusing them.

While wandering through current issues of popular male magazines, one need not be scientific to conclude that pasted on the glossy cover of every men's magazine are depicted three major issues of interest for men; magazines relating to health, fashion, and other themes feature headlines focus around power, money, and sex. For all of us are interested in learning the ability to acquire these three elements—even Christians secretly harbor great interests in the acquisition of power, money and sex. Could it be possible that this world has marketed us a false happiness, that when we aspire to attain we leave with something subordinate that glistens in the light but dissipates in the night? To be sure, power, money, and sex in and of themselves are not the greatest foes, but we must not buy into the myth of their promised fulfillment. Anything sought other than God will always leave us strangely depleted and deeply disappointed.

I will never forget when the famous and infamous Deion Sanders— depending on who you ask—walked into my office and sat crunched in a chair, looking down at the floor. He was dressed in a jogging suit with a baseball cap pressed down upon his scull. There was no neon in his eyes, no excitement in his gait. And this time it was not prime time in his life. A blind man could see his pain. Neither his Mercedes, his sprawling mansion, his jaguar, nor his Lamborghini had succeeded in bringing him the fulfillment that they had all suggested. To be sure it all glittered, but as my grandmother so aptly taught me, all that glitters is not gold. So he comes to us now with a wealth of experience, a depth of depression, and a diamond and gold encrusted hand that reached beyond CDs, stocks, and mutual funds, and reached toward heaven to claim the greater riches that cannot be calculated. Now, for the first time in a long time he smiles even when there are no cameras.

I watched Deion transform from session to session, raise his head out of the slumps of his shoulders, recapture the gleam out of his eye, and regain a boyish smile that no sports camera had been able to capture. His goal of gold had failed to score, and his defeat was deeper than any could realize; but, the greater the defeat the stronger the victory. I have often been asked what I used to win him. I always smile and respond that the greatest tool that any of us could use is the simplicity of love, the venerability of acceptance, and the old-fashioned gospel that salvages the shipwrecked lives of all men that would dare to entertain it.

Now, this is enough of my meandering through concepts and ideas. Who can tell a man's story better than the man himself? When the Pharisees came to the parents of a blind boy who had received his sight under the touch of the master himself, his parents pointed to their son and said, "He is of age; ask him: he shall speak for himself," (John 9:21, KJV). Today, ladies and gentlemen, as the senior pastor of the Potter's House in Dallas, Texas, I do not need to speak for Deion Sanders; I speak in the spirit of those aged parents whose son received a miracle so noted that the dignitaries gathered to question its authenticity. Deion Sanders is of age, turn the page and let him speak for himself.

—T.D. JAKES

PART I

chapter one

MY DATE WITH DESTINY

I was nauseous and out of it. I vaguely remember my Uncle Marvin and his wife coming in to see me in the hospital, but not much else. I didn't know what they were doing there, but at some point somebody came in and said, "Mr. Sanders, your wife is on the way." Apparently somebody had called Carolyn and she was flying in from Dallas. So I drifted off to sleep again, and the next thing I knew Carolyn was there and they were making arrangements to take me home on Jerry Jones's private plane.

In fact I had been injured in the first game of the NFC play-offs against Carolina, the first week of January 1997, in a fall that didn't appear to be all that serious. Most people watching the game on TV or up in the stands probably thought I would just get up and shake it off as I usually did. I barely touched the ground, barely hit my head, but the way I fell was bad. So suddenly there I was, realizing I had a serious injury, and the next thing I knew I was on my knees and not too sure which way was up.

Like most professional players, I have a lot of pride, and I have this thing about nobody ever having to carry me off the football field. No matter how badly I might be hurt, I've always wanted to be able to make it to the sidelines on my own. But I was out there on the field, down on my knees in a daze, surrounded by players from the opposing team, and I finally said to somebody standing there, "Hey, fellas, somebody show me where the sideline is." And my friend Eric Davis, who I had played with the year before in San Francisco, pointed over to one side and he said, "It's over there, Prime."

So I made it over there and immediately I was on my knees right down beside the bench, but I knew: *Man, something's wrong. Something's really wrong!* I was saying to the trainers and coaches who had gathered around me, "Just give me one play, man, and I'll be back in there. Just one play." But they could see that wasn't about to happen. I was out, and it didn't get much better after that.

The next thing I knew, I was out of there. Whenever I think about it now I can vaguely remember being carried out on the cart, being transported off the field and to the dressing room, barely opening my eyes. And all the Carolina fans were just cheering and clapping like they'd got religion because I'd been knocked out of the game. Michael Irvin had been hurt early in the first half, and now I was out. So the local fans were beginning to think they would be advancing to the next round of the playoffs. And the next thing I remember was them cutting my uniform off me in the hospital. I don't even remember the ride to the hospital in the ambulance.

I don't remember anything about the plane ride back to Dallas, but I remember my homeys bringing me into my house and laying me out on the bed. I had to wait a couple of days for the swelling to go down in my right eye, but as soon as it subsided enough they brought in a specialist and he performed surgery on me.

I didn't think of it at the time, but there was a spiritual object lesson in all of that. When you're lying flat on your back, you need to start looking up. But I didn't have the insight to do that at the time. Instead, I kept looking right and left and anywhere but up. It's like I was just running from all the circumstances in my life. The Lord was still trying to get my attention, but I never saw Him. I was too busy looking at myself and all my own problems.

My hair was growing long, I had a two-week growth of beard, and I hadn't been out of the bedroom in all that time. Carolyn was there by my side most of the time, and my grandmother came up from Florida to help take care of me. But one day I woke up and there was nobody in the room and that got me upset.

I picked up the phone and called down to the front of the house and said, "Where's Carolyn?" I was starting to get hungry, but I could only make it as far as the bathroom and back on my own. And the pressure of lying on one side of my face all the time was just tremendous.

Whoever answered the phone in the kitchen told me, "Carolyn has gone to school."

I said, "She what?"

They said, "She went to school. She said she had a class."

I couldn't believe my ears. I said, "She what? She went to school?!" I knew she had been taking classes at one of the local universities, but I thought, *Man, I'm not believing this!* So I yelled, "How can she think about going to class when I'm lying here in this condition? I can't even move back here!"

That was it. Something inside of me just snapped. The idea that my wife would take off and go back to her classes like that just tore it for me. All I could think of at that moment was that there was something in her life more important to her than I was, and I couldn't deal with that.

Within a few days I started coming around a little bit. My eye was still sore, but the surgery had fixed the problem and it would just be a matter of time until the swelling and the irritation dissipated. I had a black patch over one eye and I just hung around the house for weeks, waiting for things to get back to normal. I was feeling better and getting a little stronger as each day passed. Then one day I decided I had to get out of there, so I got on a plane and flew down to New Orleans for the Super Bowl. I just wanted to be someplace where I could hang out with my old friends and have a good time.

Even though I couldn't see out of my right eye, that didn't stop me. I went down there and relaxed and kicked it with my friends. It was while I was there at the Super Bowl that I decided I was going to play baseball that year.

I was running. I was hurting. I had plenty of money and everything else a man could want, but I was desperately empty inside. The football season had been emotionally crushing. The Cowboys had made it to the play-offs as a Wild Card team that year, but the loss to Carolina ended any hopes we may have had of a return trip to the Super Bowl. We finished the season with 11 wins and 7 losses, just a year after we had won Super Bowl XXX. So I didn't want to be in Dallas for a while, and I didn't want to be anywhere near Carolyn anytime soon.

I was upset with Carolyn, but I was even more upset with myself and I didn't want to be around the house. That's why I made up my mind to go play baseball. I needed a new challenge, so I decided I'd move back down to training camp in Florida for a while, then go on from there back up to my apartment in Cincinnati, and I'd just get my life back on track by myself.

The day I left the house in Dallas, I carried my bags down to the car and as I passed Carolyn in the hallway I said to her, "I know you'll be happy when I'm gone. I bet you just can't wait until I'm out of here!" She didn't say anything, but she just stared at me with this look in her eyes. I stopped and said good-bye to the kids, gave each of them a big hug and a kiss, and then I left. I flew down to the Reds training camp at Plant City, Florida, just outside Tampa, and later I heard that Carolyn had packed up and left. She left the house the next day after I had gone and nobody knew for sure where she went. My mother had to come up from Fort Myers to look after the kids.

Breaking Up

I tried to put all that stuff behind me and get ready for baseball season, but the first thing I discovered was that I couldn't see very well. I had to open up my stance at the plate so I could get a better look at the pitches coming at me. If I looked straight ahead with both eyes, I could see fine. But my vision from the side was not good at all. I remember doing outfield drills, and I was really nervous. I was afraid I was going to miss one or get hit again and that would be the end of it. I couldn't see, and it was a frightening feeling.

Nobody ever knew it. I couldn't just open up and tell everybody what I was going through—probably because I wasn't willing to admit my weakness. So I just kept working and practicing until I finally played through it. There were a few people who were saying, "Oh, he's not hitting like he used to," and stuff like that. Not like I used to be a Barry Bonds or anything, but they could see I was off my game. Finally, little by little, my sight started returning until eventually I was back to where I used to be.

The situation with my family was at a breaking point, but one particular memory stands out during that time. Just before camp got under way, I went home to Fort Myers for a visit with my family, and while I was there I decided to drive down to Miami to check in with David Eden, the guy who makes my alligator dress shoes. So I asked my mother, my little sister, and my stepfather to come with me and we would all ride down together in the limousine.

I thought that would be a good way for us all to spend some time together. But as we were driving along I realized, *We haven't been together like this since I was a kid. In fact, we hadn't even been in the same car going anywhere together since I was a baby.* Two weeks after that trip, my stepfather died. Even though I wasn't walking with God at the time, it was like God had given us that time together so we'd have those memories of spending one last good time together before he passed away. It was the first and last time we ever made a trip like that.

But the same day that I viewed my stepfather's body in Florida, Carolyn had me served with divorce papers on the field at training camp in Plant City. The effect of those two things hitting at the same time was devastating. Carolyn had to have known about my stepfather's death, and she knew the pain I was in. But it was like the football injury all over again—I was down on the field and couldn't get up on my own. I thought, *Oh, God, let me just get this thing back together.* But there was no answer. I was going to have to go through every bit of it.

So I was running on empty, but I had to keep acting like I was the life of the party. Everybody depended on me for that. I was supposed to be the catalyst of the team. I was like the Energizer bunny. I had to keep going and going. I was supposed to keep my energy and my attitude together, but I was barely holding on. Everybody else got time to recuperate now and then, but I had to stay up so everyone else could stay up. At least, that's how I felt. I was just running and running. I'd go fishing after practice, trying to find some peace of mind, but I was tore down inside and nobody around me knew it.

By the time the baseball season opened, it was obvious that I was on my way to having one of the greatest seasons of my career. I was just tearing them up. At the same time, I was trying to get my family back together, but

Carolyn wanted no part of it. I could understand that, with all the things I'd done before. But it stung me and kept me upset all the time.

As the days and weeks dragged on, I became seriously disturbed. My uncle Billy was living with me at the time and he could see me deteriorating before his eyes. I know that had to be painful for him. Billy has always stood by me through thick and thin, and he's the kind of guy who would take a bullet for me if it ever came to that. I was about to lose my mind, missing my kids more than anything. I was on the phone every day, pleading with Carolyn to come on up to Cincinnati and bring the kids, but she wouldn't do it. And to make matters worse, she told everybody she was going to a wedding shower, but word came back to me through some friends that she was going to a lot of NBA games and hanging out with some guys, and just lying about what she was really doing.

So I was in a bad situation. I was on the brink of having the best year of my professional baseball career, but my stepfather had just passed away, my wife was divorcing me, and it was all over the newspapers that my family life was coming apart. After a few weeks, I couldn't even get Carolyn to take my phone calls anymore, and I began to think that it was over for me and, without realizing how bad off I was, I became suicidal.

I called one more time and asked Carolyn to bring the kids but she flatly refused and said some very hurtful things. It was obvious that I wasn't one of her priorities. Later that day, angry, half dazed, half crazy, feeling empty inside, I was driving down the side of the highway and I came to the point where I was looking down off this drop-off about forty or fifty feet. It's still very hard for me to talk about, even now, but I wanted it to be over. I even went to the point of writing out a will in longhand, telling my people what I wanted each of them to have when I was gone.

I already had a will, of course, but I wanted them to know what was going on inside of me and what had brought me to this point. I guess it's ironic that even as I was sitting there in my car, boiling over with anger for this woman who wouldn't even come and bring my kids, I still planned to give her and the children the majority of my assets.

I didn't know what I was doing. I hadn't been drinking or taking drugs or doing anything like that. I've never done any of those things in my whole life. Still, I wasn't thinking clearly at the moment. I actually came to the point of parking my car on the side of the road after a baseball game, thinking about what I was going to do, and around four o'clock in the morning driving to this place where I was going to end it all.

As I was sitting there, thinking, crying, arguing with myself, a policeman came up and tapped on the window and asked me if I was okay. I rolled down the glass and told him everything was cool, and he ended up asking me for an autograph, not even realizing what was going on inside my head.

I'm sure he wouldn't have believed what I was thinking of doing if I'd told him. But after he drove away, I got back on the highway and drove to another spot downtown. I was sitting there thinking about running off a cliff, knowing that the lake was down there and I'd end up drowning myself. About that time another policeman came up and asked me the same thing. Once again, I assured him that everything was fine.

Finally I went back home and got showered, but with all that stuff going on I hadn't slept in three days. No sleep whatsoever. I'd lost ten pounds, but nobody noticed or said anything. I was still playing my position, hitting well, and doing pretty good overall, but I was starting to slide—down and down and down.

I remember sitting on the bench one day and emptying a whole bottle of Tylenol 3 capsules into my mouth right in front of the whole team, and the players acted as if they didn't even see it. I was just crying out for somebody to talk to me, to ask me about my situation, to care that I was dying inside, but who could have imagined that I was in so much pain. People were saying that I was a sort of figurehead of the team, and nobody would have thought for a minute that I was losing it. They depended on me.

Over the Top

By that time my attorney, Eugene Parker, and my aunt Scoodie had come down to see me, but I couldn't bring myself to talk about it even with them. I just kept saying, "Hey, I'm fine. I'm cool." But I called Carolyn one more time and this time she promised to come down and bring the kids. I got really excited and waited for them expectantly, but she didn't show up. Obviously she had changed her mind and didn't bother to tell me. Or maybe it was because she was at the NBA Playoff game between the Chicago Bulls and the Miami Heat, as my friends told me. But whatever her reasons, at that point I just went ballistic. I started turning over all the tables in my apartment, kicking over the chairs, and I went running out of the house.

Eugene was there at the time and I'm sure he thought I'd totally flipped out. I ran downstairs to the garage to get my car, but Eugene came running over to me and he said, "Deion, wait a minute, man. I'm coming with you!"

I looked him in the eyes and said, "Eugene, you've got five kids. Where I'm going, you don't even need to go." Well, that really scared him, so he jumped in front of my car and blocked the door so I couldn't get in. I tried to push him out of the way, but he resisted and we scuffled around there for a few minutes. Finally I broke away and ran across to the highway. I remember standing there on the edge of the road with cars whizzing by me at 50 or 60 miles an hour, and I was thinking, "This is it! I should jump in front of one of these cars right now!"

The thought scared me so bad I started shaking. But I didn't want to do it that way. Too messy; too cruel to whoever hit me. So I ran down the road, found a phone booth, and I called Carolyn one more time, but she still hadn't moved. It was like she was playing some kind of game with me, pushing me, goading me into something. If she was my wife and knew anything about me at all, I felt like she should have known what I was going through. After all, we had been together nine years already; surely she must have known that this was very serious for me, like nothing before or since. But she wouldn't budge, and she was just taking her time.

I slammed down the receiver and ran back toward the house, but I could see my attorney standing there at the front of the garage, waiting for me to come back. So I slipped around the back way, ducked into the garage and got into the car, then came barreling out of the garage and nearly ran over Eugene as I was coming out the door. As soon as I was out of the driveway, I punched up the radio as loud as I could and, of all things, the song that came on was Kirk Franklin's "Conquerors," which is this powerful song about overcoming adversity through the power of God's love.

I knew the song already and I really liked it, but I remember thinking, *Oh, yeah! what kind of conqueror am I?* There I was, driving 70 miles an hour down the highway with this song blasting away, and I was just looking for a spot, looking for a spot, until finally I came back to the same spot where I had been the first time.

I yanked the wheel to one side and pulled the car off the road and skidded to a stop in the loose gravel, sending up a cloud of dust. I hesitated for no more than a second or two, built up my nerve, and then put the accelerator to the floor and shot over the edge of the cliff ready to end it all. That beautiful custom-made sports car blasted into midair and seemed to hang there, suspended for a split moment in time, before it nosed down and started its crazy downward plunge.

It was the end of everything, and from that moment on nothing would ever be the same.

chapter two

FINDING MYSELF

How had I come to such a low point in my life? Deion Sanders! Prime Time! Mr. Millionaire Athlete and all that. I've wondered many times since that fateful day what really brought me to that point. How could I have made it to the top of my game in both baseball and football, with so much success, so much money and fame, with commercials and endorsements with my face all over them running on every channel during the season, and then drive off a cliff like that? What had happened to me? Where had I gone wrong?

To answer the question I needed to go back in time, because my problems didn't start that night. They started in another time and another place, and a long time ago. When I think about my life, growing up in Fort Myers, Florida, going through school and all the various sports programs, I realize that my life was always filled with promise and potential. It wasn't an easy life, but I had a purpose and a sense of direction.

There were lots of kids around my house when I was growing up—cousins, neighbors, friends from school and sports. I was touched by all of them, but the most important influences on my attitudes and behaviors when I was growing up were my mother, my grandmother, and one of my Pop Warner football coaches, a fellow named Dave Capel, who was always a man of integrity. He's still a close personal friend.

My mother had been raised in the church as a child and she believed it was important for me to be brought up that way, too, so she made sure I was in church on Sundays. Even if she wasn't there herself—which she wasn't a lot of times because of the work she did—she still made arrangements to get me to Sunday school and church. I never considered myself a Christian exactly. It wasn't that deep. But I was a sort of superficial believer. I had been exposed, and somewhere down inside of me the things I learned in church and Sunday school must have influenced the way I looked at the world.

We went through some hard times in those early years. My mother worked very hard to raise me right, and she did what she could to keep me on the right track. That wasn't always easy, raising a boy like me, a kid who was obviously on a fast track. Most of the time she worked two jobs to provide us a good living and buy me nice clothes and all the things I needed to be a normal kid. Despite all the negative stuff you hear these days about kids being raised in the projects by single mothers, I wasn't a bad kid and I didn't get into trouble—at least not very often. My mother would never put up with bad behavior.

But even as I say that, and even as I remember all the good times we had growing up, I also have to mention one time when I was thrown in jail and my mother just left me there. It was summertime and a bunch of us neighborhood boys were playing around, and not much was going on. We were bored, just kicking it like kids do, and before long we started prowling around this old vacant building down the street. At some point, somebody threw a rock and broke out a window, and then we all jumped in and started doing the same thing.

Now, we weren't being malicious exactly, we were just bored. Throwing rocks at a run-down old building seemed innocent enough. But I guess the noise of breaking glass caught somebody's ear, and before long a police car pulled up and the whole bunch of us were picked up, packed up, and taken down to the police station. As it turned out, I was playing Pop Warner football with the son of the police chief at the time, so they knew I wasn't really a bad kid. But the officers decided it would be a good idea to put the fear of the Lord into us, and they just went ahead and took us all down to jail.

After we had been there for a little while, the desk sergeant got on the phone and called our mothers and told them to come down and pick us up. The whole thing was over in a couple of hours; but, unfortunately, that wasn't the end of it. My mother had been standing out in front of our house talking to one of the neighbors when the squad car full of boys drove by, and she thought to herself, *I wonder who those boys are in that police car? I wonder what they've been up to?* It never crossed her mind that one of those young hoodlums might be her own son.

When the desk sergeant called our house a little while later and told her what had happened, Mother was really upset. She was angry at me for getting into trouble that way. But mainly she was upset because she had tried so hard to raise me right and she knew that something like that could hurt my chances. She thought I should have known better than to go along with that kind of mischief, so she did something a little unusual.

She said to the police officer, "Okay, I'll come and get him in a little while. He really should know better than that, and I'm sorry he got involved in it. But I need to know something first."

"Yes, ma'am," he said. "What's that?"

"Do you have an empty jail cell down there?"

"An empty cell?" he asked, obviously surprised by her question. "Well, yes, ma'am," he said. "I'm sure we do. But why do you ask?"

"I want you to put Deion in one of those jail cells and just hold him there for a while. Can you do that? Just let him sit there for a while and think about what he's done. I'll be down to pick him up later on."

The officer laughed and agreed to lock me up for a while, and when he put me in the cell he made out like I was going to prison for the rest of my life. Later, when my mother arrived, I was practically in shock. "Mom, Mom!" I yelled when she came in the door. "Where have you been? I thought they were going to keep me here forever!"

But the look in my mother's eyes didn't make me feel any better. She came in and put her hands on her hips and looked at me the way she always did when I did something bad, and she said, "Deion Sanders, if you're big enough to break out windows in a building like that, then you're big enough to spend your time in jail." I didn't say another word about it.

So the officer opened the cell door and Mother took me by the arm and led me straight to the car, and when we got to our house she said, "Now before you ever do anything like that again, Deion Luwynn

Sanders, I want you to remember what can happen to boys who tear up other people's property." It was a lesson I would never forget. But when we got inside the house, she had one more lesson in mind, and I got a spanking I would never forget either. I found out later that some of my friends got the same thing from their parents.

Lessons like that don't fade away quickly.

By the time I was seven years old, I already knew I had a gift from God. I was able to run faster than anybody my age. I usually hung around with guys three or four years older than I was, so I was used to competing with guys bigger and stronger than I was, and I was used to beating them. Whenever I competed or communicated with people my own age I was always above the crowd. I was something above the norm, and I wasn't a follower. When I was with a group of kids, wherever I was, I would always take the lead. I never walked behind, I was in the front. I was a creator and innovator, even as a child.

I always liked sports and games when I was a little kid, and I really like playing ball—any kind of ball. My mom says that when I was four years old I was always pestering her to take me down to the park to get on one of the local teams. She didn't know how old I had to be to play in a league, so she put if off for a while. But I kept pushing her, saying, "Mom, just take me down there because I might be old enough now!"

When she took me down there to check it out, sure enough they said, "Sorry. He's not old enough." So I said, "How old do I have to be?" And they said I could start playing T-ball at age five. As soon as I turned five, she signed me up, and that's how I got my start in sports.

By this time my grandmother had moved up from Georgia to be nearby, and her house was right across the street from the practice field. She would look after me during the day and make sure I got across the road to T-ball practice every morning. That was fine for a while but I couldn't wait until it was time to play football, but they told me I had be eight years old to sign up for football. So, again, we waited. And as soon as I turned eight, my mother carried me over and signed me up for the city leagues.

That was the beginning. I played city-league football that year, but when it came time to go back the next season, I told my mother, "Mom, I don't want to play down there anymore. I want to play with a big-time team!" Nine years old and I was ready to go. We had heard about the

Rebels by that time, and they were the really good team in Fort Myers, so she took me to meet Coach Capel and he took me on his squad.

She took me to the first team meeting, then to the first practice, then to the first game, and one thing just naturally led to another. But it wasn't long before the coaches started seeing something in me and they were saying, "Hey, this kid is pretty good!" I never went to any baseball camps, sports seminars, or anything like that. It was always just "look and learn." I'd look and see what the other kids were doing and I learned quickly. Nobody had to show me anything twice. But I was a perfectionist. I never wanted to be mediocre in anything. I wanted to be "the best" at whatever I put my hand to, and I would spend as much time as it took to learn how things should be done.

Part of that was because I had seen what happens to people who settled for second or third best in life. My biological father left when I was just six years old. He was the original Prime Time, and he was something else! His name was Mims Sanders but everybody just called him Daddy Buck. I continued to see him off and on. We weren't very close in those days, but I knew he cared for me.

I called him "Buck," and he was proud of me and encouraged me in sports. He came to my games, and he always let me know he was proud of me. We would eventually grow a lot closer after I was grown, but I was afraid of him in the beginning. I just didn't know him very well.

My mother and I were on our own for quite a while. But a few years after Daddy Buck and my mother seperated, my mother married a man named Will Knight, so then I also had a stepfather in my life. But you know, I learned alot more from the wrongs my fathers did than from the rights. My biological father used drugs, and my stepfather used alcohol.

To this day I've never messed with either of those and I never will. Not once in my entire life have I even tried any of those things. Never smoked a cigarette, never took a chance with any of it. I knew what it could do. I had already seen what those things did to destroy my fathers, and I learned from seeing the results of their bad behavior.

How I Got My Speed

Growing up in my old neighborhood taught me all kinds of things about life, and I give at least part of the credit for my success in athletics to the place I came from. Because that's where I got my speed. People usually say you inherit speed and athletic ability from your parents. People always told me the reason I could run fast was because my biological father, Daddy Buck, was such a fast runner. But I'm not sure about that.

What I do know is that we lived down at the end of Henderson Avenue in Fort Myers, and right across the street from us was this huge graveyard that seemed to go on forever. If you walked down to the end of our driveway, you could see graveyard in both directions. I've heard people say, "The longer your driveway the longer your money," and we had a very short driveway at that time, so maybe that tells you how we lived. But if I was standing on the street in front of my house, on the right was a graveyard. Across the street there was another graveyard. Two blocks down the street there was graveyard on both sides of the street.

You never really get used to something like that, especially if you're a young boy with a vivid imagination. But I found out that living in a place like that could affect you in other ways, too. I used to go down to the recreation center to play ball every day after school, but coming home at night I had to walk right past all those graveyards. No matter which way I came, I had to pass graveyards! That was pretty scary, and whenever I came home after dark, which was most of the time, I could imagine all sorts of spooky things coming out of there to get me.

So one day I came up with this plan—a plan for whenever I had to go home after dark. I knew that speed was my best resource, so when I left the recreation center I would walk down to the corner just before the first graveyard and wait until a car came down the street with its lights on. Then, just as the car was passing, I would take off running in the same direction as fast as I could go. I would try to keep up with the car—to keep up with the lights, anyway—until I made it all the way home.

I sprinted the whole way practically every single night, running as fast as I could go! So from as early as six or seven years old—and really all my growing-up years—I was constantly running like that, and I say that's where I got my speed. Racing against the dark!

Speed was very important to me and it helped me succeed in sports. There were lots of coaches and teachers at the schools I attended who saw something in me and encouraged me. They helped me to see that I could be somebody someday. They showed me that if I worked at it I could do something with my life. Unfortunately, there were also a few coaches and teachers who never believed in me, who put me down, or who just told me I was headed for trouble. For whatever reasons, there always seemed to be a few people who wanted to put me down and break my spirit, but I wasn't about to let that happen.

I grew up fast because it was just my mother and me for quite a while, but back in those days I think kids were more responsible. When I was six and seven years old, my mother would lay out my clothes before she left for work, pin the house key on my outfit, and I would get myself up, bathe myself, fix my own cereal, and go to school by myself. Today they'd call that child abuse. You couldn't get away with that anymore! But that's the way it was, and I think one of the reasons I matured early was because she trusted me and demanded a lot from me. My mother put the burden on me and I accepted it. I suppose some kids wouldn't do that. But that's how we made it by.

I also grew up with sports. My mother signed me up for everything from swimming lessons to Pee Wee baseball to Pop Warner football, and just about anything else that sounded promising. I was an outstanding runner and I was hitting home runs at eight years old, and all that kind of stuff. I could relate to Jackie Robinson even as a kid because most of the time I was the only black player in my league. I was the one opening doors for all the other black kids who would come after me. Those were important times in my life. I learned a lot from sports, and I was able to use my athletic abilities to get ahead in other areas as well.

We would play football down in the 'hood, in the projects, running with milk cartons between the apartments. Yes, milk cartons! That's what we used for the ball because that was all we had. My mother knew that sports would be important for me someday, so she encouraged me and helped me get started. But she also realized that I wasn't going to go any-where in sports if I just hung around with the neighborhood kids playing sandlot ball, or if I just played with the local teams.

They had a lot of good players down there, but their teams didn't have the same pressure to win like the teams across town. And they didn't have the same opportunities either. So my mother made arrangements for me to play over there, and she would drive me across the bridge to a better part of town where I would be playing on teams with mostly—and some-times only—white kids.

The reason I didn't play in the black community was because my mother wanted it to be more organized. I mean, the black community was organized, but if the game was supposed to start at seven o'clock, we might get started by 7:30 or 8:00. But over in the white community it was more organized, and a seven o'clock game usually started a few minutes after 7:00. So that's why she put me over there.

All those years I wound up playing football and baseball with guys from affluent families. Their parents owned businesses or were professional people of some kind. I was about the only guy on the squad who didn't have a lot of money. My mother tells a story about me coming home from a game one night and telling her what I had seen. We had just won the last big game and as a reward, one of the leaders, a white lady named Earlene Sanders who trained the girls on the cheerleading squad, invited us over to her house after the game for ice cream. And that was a real eyeopening experience.

When I got home I was so excited. "Mom, Mom!" I yelled as soon as I came in the door. My mother says my eyes were as big as saucers, and I said, "Mom, you won't even believe it! We went over to Ms. Sanders's house after the game and you won't believe how big their house is. Mom, you can put our whole house inside her house and still have room for the front yard!"

Mother just laughed. I know she understood my excitement. I had never seen anything like that before. Our lives were pretty simple, but she had been a cleaning lady in rich people's houses and other places like that, so she knew what I was talking about. She spent every day working, slaving over a hot stove, doing everything she could to help me have a better life, and that night I realized that not everybody lived the way we did.

I think that night was the first time I ever began to think that maybe we didn't always have to live that way. I told her about all the things I had seen that night, and after a few minutes I took her hand and looked her in the eye and said, very seriously, "Mom, someday I'm going be very rich. I'm going to make a whole lot of money and I'm going to buy you a big house like that. You'll never have to work another day in your life."

Maybe she believed me. Maybe she didn't. More than likely her next sentence was something like, "Yeah, that's fine and dandy, but for right now you can just get on in there and do your homework!"

But what I remember most is that my mother always did whatever she could to give me a better life, to give me a chance to succeed. She believed in me and she thought I had the skills to be a top athlete, and she believed I would do well if I could just get a chance to play. I figured that if I played well enough and made a lot of money someday, that would be another way of saying "thank you" for all that she had done for me.

Living with Pain

Baseball was my first sport because it was the easiest to get involved with at that age. There were T-ball leagues, Pee Wees, YMCA teams, Little League, and all kinds of programs like that for kids. At the same time that I was playing baseball on my own side of town I'd be playing football across the bridge. Then at the end of baseball season each year I would wind up playing in the all-star baseball games against the same guys who were my football buddies the rest of the year. And if you think that made for some intense rivalries, you're absolutely right!

The players on the other teams were pretty good, but I was the pitcher and the lead-off hitter on our team. The guys on the other side—all white guys most of the time—would yell at me and tease me and say all kinds of crazy stuff, but since I was the lead-off batter I would start off with a double or a triple, or sometimes even a home run my first time at the plate. Then sometime during the game I would usually come through with a homer or maybe a grand slam. My last season in Little League Baseball we ended up beating the other team in the finals something like 17 to 1. Nobody thought we could do that, but we did. And I think that's when I really started making a reputation as an all-around athlete.

Even if I could make things happen on the field, I couldn't do much about some of the things that happened off the field. I remember one time when I was playing Pee Wee football, right before I moved up to the Pop Warner league, and our team had just won its division and advanced to the championship game. That was really big for us. I was the star running back on the team and everybody knew we were going to win. I mean, it was in the wind. Everybody knew it. All I had to do was show up.

It was almost a joke around Fort Myers. People would say, "Whenever Deion Sanders touches the football it's a touchdown!" And it usually was. It was automatic. But I've suffered with migraine headaches all my life— still do—and that has been a problem for me at times, especially trying to control a headache before a big game. There have been times when my head would hurt so bad I couldn't see straight. I couldn't think straight.

Couldn't do anything. And if I didn't take painkillers and go straight to bed, I would be throwing up and feeling like I was going to die.

In the youth football leagues in those days we always got dressed for the game at home. We didn't have locker rooms or anything like that, of course, and I remember the afternoon of that big game sitting there on the edge of my bed in my uniform, with my cleats on, knowing I wasn't going to be able to go to the championship game because of my headache. I felt like my head was about to explode, so my mother gave me a couple of aspirins and put me to bed. Since I couldn't make it to the game, our team got beat really bad. My guys lost, and I had the feeling that I had let the whole team down. It was a terrible feeling.

But there was no way I could have played with that kind of pain. The headache would get so bad that all I could do was go to sleep. And then most of the time when I woke up the pain would be gone. But I remember how I felt later that night, waking up, still in my uniform, and knowing that we had lost the game. I didn't have to ask. I already knew it. That happened in 1975 when I was still just seven years old. It was my second year in organized sports, and to this day it's one of the most vivid memories of those growing up years.

I wasn't the quarterback at that point. I was a running back—number 32! In fact, they called me "the juice." I would score the touchdown, get in the end zone and do the Billy "Whiteshoes" Johnson dance. Whiteshoes was at the top of his game in those days, so I'd do his dance and do the bump with the goalpost and all that kind of stuff!

For those people who think that Deion Sanders is just making all that stuff up, here's some news for you. I've been doing that stuff since 1974—high-stepping down the sideline, putting on a show. I was doing all that a long time ago! Even today some people make a lot of fuss about me dancing and strutting and all that, but my people back home will tell you, "Prime Time's been doing that stuff since the very beginning!" The Deion you see out there on Sundays didn't just happen yesterday.

Years later, when I was playing for the Atlanta Falcons, I ran into Billy "Whiteshoes" Johnson at some celebrity event and I had a chance to tell him, "Hey, man, I used to do your dance!"

He just laughed and said, "You're not telling me nothing I didn't know, man! I seen you play! I know exactly where that stuff comes from!"

That was fun. I always did have a habit of learning from the best.

chapter three

FAST AND LOOSE

I thank the Lord for the way I was brought up. I've got a hard-working mother. Quick temper, quick tongue, don't take nothing off nobody, but she's always been my partner and my friend. She's a strong black woman who talks junk, but she was my strength and my cover for most of my growing up years. She's still young, and she looks young. She doesn't look old enough to be my mother. But we were close, and we had an understanding when I was growing up, especially when I was in high school.

She knew I was mature enough to handle myself and she expected me to be responsible and do the right things. She sacrificed to make sure I was the best-dressed kid in school. I never lacked for anything I really needed, but she would do things that would teach me how to develop my own independence. A lot of mothers will go out and buy their kids clothes and decide what they're going to wear, but my mother didn't do any of that. She would give me the money and I'd go out and buy my own clothes. I had to learn to stretch my money to get the things I felt I needed. I learned a lot of responsibility that way.

We didn't have as much money as most of the people I hung around with so I used to lie and tell them my mother was a nurse down at the hospital. The truth was, she cleaned the hospital. She also worked as a cleaning woman at one of the local schools and she always worked all kinds of odd jobs to make sure we had enough money for clothes, sports equipment, or anything else I needed. My younger sister, Tracy, who is nine years younger than I am, was there, too, but by the time she came along I was already very involved in sports.

Being that far apart in age, Tracy and I each had our own separate groups of friends growing up, but we were brother and sister. We knew each other and spent quite a bit of time together. She always enjoyed coming to my games to watch me play. But I don't come from one of those homes where people say they love each other very much. I think we all knew we loved each other, but we never said it. It was just sort of understood.

And we never broke bread together either. Everybody just came and went. We ate when we ate, and we didn't have a lot of togetherness because our parents were too busy just trying to provide a living for us. There was always food and if we were hungry we just ate, but there wasn't anything like a family dinner. That wasn't happening at our house! And usually there was gonna be some cussin'! My mother was a very dominant woman, and she laid down the law.

I had a praying Christian grandmother, too. Her name is Hattie Mims, and I never heard her curse, even with all I did to provoke her. I never saw her with a man, and I never saw her get angry. I never knew her husband, my grandfather, who passed away. But I never saw her with any other man, and there's no doubt she was and is a woman of God.

I actually lived with her back and forth during those early years of my life. I'd live with Grandma for a year, then I'd be back home with my mother, because Grandmas wasn't having anymore of that. But being with Grandma was a real blessing because at her house you always knew where you stood. You had to be in at a certain time and she had definite rules. You didn't ever mess with Grandma. No way! So it was just a total blessing to be with her.

My mother also had a sister and two brothers and they've always been close to me, too. My uncle Billy, who looks after my place in Atlanta, has stood by me through thick and thin. He's a guy I look up to today when I need advice or someone to talk to. My aunt Annette Moss, nicknamed Scoodie, is also very close and she helps me with the Bible study, "Prime

Time Tuesdays," that we hold in a large church in North Dallas. Most of the time my friend Pastor David Forbes flies in from Columbus to lead it, and it's packed every Tuesday.

But there was a lot of transferring back and forth during those early years. When I was at Grandmother's house I'd go to one school; but when I was staying with my mother, it would be a different school. So there was a lot of moving around.

Pop Warner Football

I got started in Pop Warner football when I was eight—the first minute I was eligible to sign up. There were thirty-five boys on that team, and I was one of just three black kids. That was back in 1977. The name of the district team was the Rebels, and our squad was called the "Dynomites!" I played for Coach Capel for three years and we had a record of 38 wins and 1 loss.

The loss was up in North Carolina when we played for the championship game our first year. Coach says that the other team was a little bigger than we were, but I remember that the weather was freezing. It must have been ten below zero and, for a bunch of Florida boys it was pure torture. We had never played in cold weather before, and we had never played on red clay either.

That was our one loss, but two years later, in 1979, we made it back to the nationals, and this time it was in Atlanta, on red clay. I scored the first three touchdowns, and we went on to win the championship game in Pop Warner football. Coach Capel estimates that I scored about 120 touchdowns in my career on that team. I remember that there were times when it was almost embarassing for me, because as soon as they'd hand me the ball I would just take it in.

But you know, one of the interesting things about Pop Warner teams is that academics is rated on an equal basis with athletics. So at the end of every week, we all had to bring our progress reports from school, and if we didn't keep up our grades we would have to go to the locker room where Mrs. Capel would sit down with us and help us with our homework.

About every other week I would have to spend a little time in the locker room and I never liked that. It seemed like a waste of time, and I'd say, "Coach, I don't want to go in the locker room." But he would just say,

"You've got to do it, Deion, and you know you've got to keep up your grades if you want to stay on the football team."

So I would bring my books and Mrs. Capel would tutor me whenever I needed a little help. In Pop Warner, half of it is your grades. We can have eleven wins and no losses and still not make the finals if our players didn't keep up their grades. The year we won the national championship, our team had an A–average for all thirty-five boys. The year before that we had a B+ and we were fourth in the nation. But the last year I played we moved up with our grades and won all our games, and that helped us win the championship.

Coach Capel has a daughter and two sons of his own, but he always treated me like a third son. He coached for ten years on various Fort Myers teams—baseball, football, boxing—but Coach says he always remembers those three years as the best. He said to me, "I'm grateful to you, Deion, because you really made it a fun game for all of us. You know," he said, "I could coach all my life and never have another Deion Sanders." He's a great friend and he was the one who got me started. If it wasn't for Coach Capel I don't know where I'd be today.

For all my flash on the field, I was a quiet kid off the field. I had skinny legs at that time and I only weighed about eighty-five pounds. Coach says that anybody looking at me on the sideline would never have thought that I could even play the game. But as soon as I stepped onto the field, I became a different person, and I would always give 110 percent. Our opponents discovered that even a skinny kid could be tough. Coach says he knew I was going to be a good player the first year that I played on his squad. But in the second year something happened, and it was like I had turned on the afterburner.

Years later when I was playing for Coach Bobby Bowden at Florida State, we were having a team meeting before we left to play Auburn in the Sugar Bowl in 1989. We were all sitting around the meeting room and Coach Bowden was saying, "Now, none of you guys have ever played on a national championship team, but this is the year we're going to win it all."

But before he could finish the thought, I raised my hand and said, "Coach, I played on a national championship team, and we won."

Coach Bowden looked at me skeptically and he said, "Yeah, Deion? Where was that?"

I said, "Pop Warner Football. My team won the National Championship in 1979!"

Coach Bowden just laughed and said, "Okay, Deion, but we won't count that!"

Maybe Pop Warner wasn't in the same league with NCAA football, but I wanted him to know that I was playing on winning teams from the start. In fact, it's probably harder to win a national championship in Pop Warner ball than an NCAA championship—if you consider the odds. If you stop to think how many Pop Warner teams there are around the country, you realize that any team that makes it to the finals has to be a pretty determined bunch of kids.

Pop Warner Football has leagues in thirty-eight states all over the country, plus Japan and Mexico, and every year more than 270,000 kids play on Pop Warner teams. Compare that to the NFL with fewer than 1,600 active players, or the NCAA with maybe a hundred truly competitive college teams. So our victory down in Atlanta was something to be proud of. I wore number 29 at that time. I played running back, defensive safety, punted the ball, kicked the extra points, and basically did it all. And most of all, I really loved to intercept the other team's passes.

Whenever I would run the ball, the other team would try to pile on if they could catch me. But when I was on defense, I loved to intercept the ball, and then I would go out of my way knocking their players down when I was running back with the football. I remember one time after I had put a sting on about four or five of their guys, and I ran over to the sideline and yelled, "Okay, Coach, I just got my revenge for all the times they knocked me down!"

One reason Coach Capel realized that I had the instincts to play football was because whenever I would hit a defensive player, I would lower my shoulders and go right through the guy. I guess there weren't very many at that age who had the presence of mind to do that. But if I could see I was going to get tackled, I would get down and come right over them. I think that was just my way of making the opponents respect my ability.

Moving Up

From there I went on to junior high school sports, and unfortunately those years didn't make a very big impression on me, except that I do remember getting cut from the basketball team my eighth-grade year. That really hurt because I was a good basketball player. I was playing football at the same time, and football always took a lot of time. So I decided I must have got cut because I missed basketball practice so much.

They always posted the roster of the guys who made the team on the lunchroom wall where everybody could see it. I remember walking over there one day with a bunch of my homeys and we looked all over the board and my name wasn't on it. I couldn't believe it. So I just said, "Oh, man, it's just because I didn't come to practice all the time." But it was embarrassing, nevertheless.

Right then I decided I was going to have to prove something to those guys. When we got to high school, most of them wound up playing for Fort Myers High School and I went on to play for North Fort Myers. So whenever we'd play them, I'd always go for 20 or 30 points, dunk on them, and just do everything I could to let them know I didn't deserve to get cut from their team. I averaged something like 24 points per game in basketball my senior year.

I made the move up to Fort Myers High School, but I knew right away that it wasn't a good situation. The coaches at Fort Myers weren't giving me a chance to play. I mean, in my sophomore year I was still playing JV football and backing up at quarterback, and that was just crazy! The whole team knew I was better than the guy in the position.

So I made another move and transferred up to North Fort Myers, and in my first season I was fielding kickoffs and punt returns. In my junior year I started the season on the varsity string and I started at quarterback for the rest of my time there. Even if there were some doubts in the beginning, it didn't take long for just about everybody to realize that I had come to the right place.

North Fort Myers was a mostly all-white school in an all-white part of town, but I was recognized as an exceptional player from the first.

You know, that gave me a certain pleasure, knowing that the coaches who had doubted my ability at Fort Myers High were being proved wrong every time I stepped on the field. And some of the time they were on the receiving end of the evidence. The best proof of their bad judgment was when I pounded them on the gridiron or on the baseball diamond, and I did that just about every time we played.

When I first arrived at the new school, I wondered if things were going to be better for me there or whether it would just be more of the same old thing. It felt better from the start, but there was one incident that made me wonder if I'd done the right thing. I think it was my second day in school, and as I was walking across the campus I saw a piece of paper lying on the ground.

I don't know why, but for some reason I just reached down and grabbed it and tossed it up on the roof of the building. I didn't see a wastebasket or anything, so I threw it away just to get rid of it. But I guess the principal must have been looking out the window at that exact moment, because he came storming outside and called me into the building. He chewed me out for throwing paper on the roof, and then he took me down to his office and paddled me.

Now, he didn't know me. I was just this new kid and maybe he wanted to make a point. But all it did was make me angry. I said, "What's this all about?" And he said, "It's to teach you a lesson. We don't put up with that kind of behavior around here." How do you respond to something like that?

My mother was tough with me, too, but I always knew she wanted the best for me. This man didn't know me from Sammy Davis, Jr., and who knows what he was trying to say? But I just let it go. I remember thinking, *If that's how it's going to be at North Fort Myers High School, I might as well get on back to my own side of town.* Fortunately, that's not the way it was at North Fort Myers.

There were a few times when some of the kids would put me down or try to hurt me in some way. As early as eight or nine years old I was getting attention for my athletic abilities, but even then there were some people who apparently felt they had to shoot me down and hurt me and doubt my ability. But I got a lot of encouragement from my family, and I always believed in myself. I knew I was good, and I was determined I was going to do it all, and do it my way.

By the time I was a sophomore in high school, the peer pressure was really awesome. I weighed about 120 pounds at the time and I was playing varsity football. The star receiver on the team lived right behind our house on Henderson Avenue, and he was one of my good friends. He used to look out for me, but sometimes he would get into stuff that I didn't want to do.

I remember one day in particular when I needed a ride home from practice and I heard somebody saying that this other guy, who was the top defensive end on our team, had a pickup truck and he was taking my friend home. They had to go right by my house, so I asked him for a ride and he said, sure, he'd drop me off.

We all piled in the truck and headed out. Before long we crossed over the bridge to my part of town, and on the way down there these two guys lit up and started passing a joint back and forth. I thought, *Oh, man! This ain't me. I'm sitting right in the middle between these two guys, and they're going to make me smoke weed with them!* But the first thought that went through my mind was that the stench of that stuff was going to get into my clothes and my mother was going to kill me if I came into the house smelling like that. So I knew I had to make a decision right then.

Basically, I had three options: One, I could go along and get high with them, because I knew that they were going to ask me to in a second. And if I did that I would probably just fit in and be cool. Two, I could say no and make them think I was a jerk. Or three, I could just say, "Oh, no thanks, man, I had some earlier," but that would be a lie.

Well, sure enough, pretty soon they asked me if I wanted a hit and I said, "No, man, y'all just let me in the back of the truck." They didn't say anything about it. They pulled over and I crawled around to the back and rode home that way. Maybe they talked about me, I don't know. But I knew what I did was the right thing.

A few years later when I was coming up in college and the pros, I ran across one of those guys and he had become an Ida. "If Ida done this or if Ida done that I'd be where you are today." But that's how the peer pressure was when I was coming up. But I just decided I would rather stay straight and take the abuse than give in to it and waste my chances.

Showing Some Stuff

There were a couple of young ladies in high school that I wanted to get to know, but they wouldn't give me the time of day. They were sharp, fine looking, and I was just starting to get serious about girls around that time. But these two preferred to hang out with drug dealers because they had money and cars and jewelry and all that kind of stuff. But their lives were depressing.

Later when I started coming up in sports, getting a reputation as a player, on and off the field, and when my name started making the headlines practically every week, these girls who had been so hard to get a few months ago suddenly wanted to holler at me. They wanted to get with me because they realized I was going someplace.

I remember another time in high school when we had what they called "Student Day." This was a day for just goofin' around and having fun, and everybody went out to the football field and we played games and had fun. The whole school was out on the football field and there were stands set up with all kinds of refreshments that people could buy, and it was like a small school carnival.

They had all kinds of sports events that anybody could participate in, and practically the whole student body showed up for fun and games. It was just a day for kickin' it and letting go.

But at one point I noticed that all the seniors and the top guys on the track team were getting ready to run the hundred-yard dash, and I thought, *Man, I can do that!* Now I was just a sophomore and nobody thought I could run with those guys. Some of the other students knew I was a player, but nobody thought of me as "the man" or anything like that at that time.

So I just went down and lined up and ran against the best guys on the track team, and I beat every one of them by at least five yards. When it was over, they acted like it was no big deal. Some of them said, "Ah, man, we weren't really running!" But that was big for me. It was a statement, and I know the coaches didn't miss any of that.

We still had a lot of rednecks at North Fort Myers in those days, and to get to school we had to drive over from the 'hood through that part of town. I remember one afternoon after school, I was out in the parking lot talking and joking with a group of white girls, and we were having fun, telling jokes, kickin' it.

But there was this one little white girl who was just prejudiced and talking junk and giving me a hard time for no reason. She must have been thirty yards away standing there with one foot in her car, just calling me names and being obnoxious. I guess she didn't like the fact that a black guy would be standing there talking to all those white girls. But I just happened to have a football in my hand, so she made one wisecrack too many and I just drew back and threw a perfect strike. The ball hit her right square in the mouth. Everybody laughed, she shut up, and we all drove home. But that wasn't going to be the end of it.

I was the main man on the basketball team that year and we had a big game that night. I had forgotten all about the incident in the parking lot, but when we came out of the locker room onto the basketball court that evening, I looked up in the stands and it looked like a KKK meeting! Practically every redneck in Florida had showed up for the game. I thought, *Oh, man, those guys are here to hang me!* But when the principal and the coaches saw what was going on, they called the police out there and they snuck me out the back way when the game was over.

I mean, on one side of the gym you had all the blacks and they were ready to fight. On the other side were all the rednecks and they were ready to fight. And it was almost a riot. But they got me out of there and it was cool after that. But it was tense for a little while.

I remember sitting out in front of my house with some of my homeys after the game and somebody went and got a gun. I think they were probably just hoping that some of those good old boys had followed us over there. But nothing ever came of it, and the school took care of everything. But there were so many rednecks that night, man, it was like the rodeo had come to town!

chapter four

TURNING THE CORNER

L ittle by little things started picking up for me, and I had a very successful and enjoyable high school career. On the athletic field I was doing everything right, and in the classroom I was able to do as much as the teachers expected of me, and a little more. I wasn't an "A" student by any means, but I always kept pretty good grades. As a matter of fact, my most prized trophy from high school was the one I got for having the highest grade point average on the team. So academics were always important to me.

My favorite subject in school was English. I could always articulate what I wanted to say. I could write stories and use words to capture other people's imagination, and one particular teacher, Mrs. Fleming, my high school English teacher, was very helpful and very important to me.

She always encouraged me, and she always made sure I had somebody to help me with my studies so I could make it through. She was a real blessing. Whenever I go back there now—which I do fairly often—I always go see Mrs. Fleming, to get her tickets to the Super Bowl and things like that.

The one really negative experience I recall during my time there was being kicked off the team my junior year. Like most schools, they had a rule at North Fort Myers that if you were ever suspended for any reason you'd automatically be kicked off the team. I never thought much about that rule because I wasn't a bad kid and I didn't do things to get into trouble. Besides, I was the starting quarterback and I was doing everything I was expected to do. I was a standout on the field, and making good grades in all my subjects. So I thought I had everything on track, but there was always something to trip me up.

With athletics and everything else I was doing, I didn't have a lot of free time, but I always found a way to do my schoolwork. One afternoon I went to the school library to check out some books and do some research for a report I was working on. But one of the women who worked in the library just started giving me a hard time. To this day I don't know what set her off, but I was trying to do my work, looking for some books or magazines, and she kept giving me lip, scolding me about this and that and everything else.

Finally I said I'd heard just about enough. I became rebellious and blasted her back. I said some things, and that was all she needed to hear. She marched me down to the principal's office and later the same day I was officially suspended from school.

The coach told me later it was the hardest thing he ever had to do, but he kicked me off the team with only three games left in the season. Even though he knew it meant the end of the team's winning season, he did it. He followed the rules and disciplined me, and I realize now that the experience taught me some important lessons.

But best of all, that man, Coach Ron Hoover, became a good friend and has been close to me and my family ever since. The suspension didn't last very long, and when the new school year started I resumed my position as quarterback and wide receiver and had an outstanding season throughout my senior year. Our team did extremely well that year.

Eventually, however, my success on the field led to one of the toughest decisions I would ever have to make: Would I accept an offer from the Kansas City Royals to play professional baseball, and make a lot of money, or would I accept one of the offers I had received to go on to college and play football and baseball on scholarship?

For most of my senior year our mailbox was constantly jammed full of recruiting letters from colleges all over the country. Coaches called and wrote me practically every day, wanting me to come play football or baseball on full scholarship. At first that was exciting, getting all that mail. I was like a kid at Christmas thinking about all the places I could go and the teams I might end up playing for. But after a while it became almost a nightmare.

Every day another stack of letters, and they all said the same things. Now and then some college recruiter would call or come by the house, wanting me to come to his school. At that point my mother and I realized we needed to make a decision.

I had been a standout in baseball, football, and basketball, and I was being drafted to play baseball for the Royals. Not a lot of people know about that, but I thought about it for a long time. Then, after looking at everything and thinking about the long-range potential of playing baseball or going to college, I finally decided not to go pro at that time.

First of all, they weren't offering me enough money to make it worthwhile. But second, I knew I really wanted to play football. Football was my best sport, and I wanted to see how good I could be. I thought I'd like playing for Coach Bobby Bowden and the Florida State Seminoles. So eventually I turned down the Royals' offer and went on to college. By that time I was pretty sure I was on my way.

Some Good Advice

Being drafted out of high school to play baseball for the Kansas City Royals was a real honor, and I was proud they made the offer. It was ironic, in a way, because when I was still in elementary school, the Royals' spring training facility was only a mile or so from our school, and I used to skip school and go over there and hustle balls outside the ballpark whenever the team was in town. That's how I made my spending money, hustling balls that came over the fence.

I could outrun everybody, so if they hit a ball over the fence, most of the time I'd be the first one there to get it. I carried a big tube sock around with me, and pretty soon I'd have a sock full of balls. When the game started, I'd sell baseballs to the fans as they were coming into the park. And then, being the businessman that I was, I'd take the best ball, get it autographed by the whole team, and I'd give that one to my teacher, so she would cover for me for leaving school.

It was ironic that, all those years later, that would be the team that ended up drafting me out of high school. I don't exactly remember the terms of their deal, but it seems like they were offering me a $75,000 bonus to come out of high school. But it was such a major decision, and it involved some potentially life-changing choices, so I didn't think I should be in too big a hurry to make up my mind.

Oddly enough, the best advice I got when I was going through all that was from the late Dick Hauser, who was the manager for the Royals at that time. I had been a Royals fan practically all my life, ever since I had shagged balls in the parking lot, so I didn't like the idea of refusing their offer. I was already beginning to think that going to college was the right thing to do, but one day as I was wrestling with it, I went down to the ballpark to watch the Royals work out and they let me come down on the field and I got to speak with Dick Hauser.

What a wonderful guy! In all our official discussions, Mr. Hauser would tell me what a great organization the Royals had put together and what an outstanding tradition they had, and all that kind of thing. But when I talked to him privately, on the field and not in any boardroom or any kind of planned meeting, he said, "Deion, don't do it."

I couldn't believe he was saying that, but I could tell he was being honest with me. He put his hand on my shoulder and said, "Go on to college and get your degree." I was really impressed that he seemed to understand my situation and wanted me to make the right choice, not just for the team but for me. He told me, "If you're good enough to get drafted out of high school, you'll be good enough to get drafted out of college. And while you're at college you'll have a chance to see just how good you can be at football."

He was about the only person I met during that time who seemed concerned that I would make not just a lot of money but the right decision for my life. Unfortunately, I think the Royals management developed a grudge against me because I didn't sign with them at that time— especially John Sherholtz, the general manager. I never said anything about it to anybody, but it was Dick Hauser's advice that really gave me the confidence to make my decision. And I know now it was the right one.

But I still think about all the young guys just coming up who don't get that kind of advice, or maybe they don't take it, so they don't get an education and some of them don't last long enough in the pros to ever make a difference. Some of them wind up on the streets or sweeping warehouse docks because they took the easy way instead of taking care of the basics.

But Dick Hauser taught me an important lesson. And, besides that, he also gave me the baseball glove that I used all through my senior year in high school.

All during the rest of that year, I received dozens of offers from colleges all over the country, encouraging me to come play for them. Whenever a letter would come to the house from any of the big out-of-state colleges, I would show them to my mom and say, "Look here, Mom! They want me to come up there and play!" I couldn't really imagine what it would be like to go so far from home to play football and baseball, but I liked the sound of it, and I must have looked at those letters a hundred times thinking about which one I should choose.

That was very exciting, but being a realist and a very practical person, my mother said one day, "Now look here, Deion. Those schools you're so excited about are a million miles from here, and if I'm going to ever see you play football I'd have to fly there on an airplane."

"Yeah, I know that, Mama," I said. "You can do that. You're not afraid to fly on an airplane are you?"

"No, of course not," she said. "But you know I can't afford to go flying halfway across the country every single weekend just to see you play football!"

She was right, of course, but I hadn't considered that. So she said, "If you're going to pick one of those colleges, then pick one here in Florida so I can drive there to see you. That's the only way I can come to the games."

So that's what I did. I had friends who were planning on going to the University of Miami. But I didn't want to go to Miami. I knew some other guys who were going to Florida, but I didn't want to play for the Gators either. So I finally decided I would go to Florida State. They had been nice to me and my family. I liked the school, the team, the coaches. And they had a winning tradition. So that was my choice.

The recruiters from FSU were offering me a full athletic scholarship and a chance to play baseball at the same time if I wanted to. Besides that, it was only four hundred miles from Fort Myers to Tallahassee, so my mother and my family could drive up and watch me play every weekend when we were playing at home. It was a long enough drive that she had to go on Friday and come back Saturday night, but it was the best choice for everybody.

I wanted to be very respectful of the Royals, so one day I went down to the training camp and met some of the coaches. But after I decided to take Dick Hauser's advice and turn down the contract, I announced my decision to the media, and I started getting ready to make the move up to Tallahassee to start my new life at Florida State University. I couldn't wait to get started.

Making Adjustments

Coach Bobby Bowden wrote a book in 1994, *More Than Just a Game*, and in it he talked about his experiences as a coach and a Christian. I think that's really great, and now that I'm writing my own book I can appreciate what he was trying to do in a way I couldn't understand at that time. I wasn't walking with the Lord when I was playing at FSU and that sort of thing didn't really mean much to me then.

I used to go to FCA meetings, the Fellowship of Christian Athletes, but the FCA wasn't really in me. I would just go because my friends were there. It was just a bunch of guys, and most of them were going for the same reason I was. I wasn't living right. I knew I wasn't. But it didn't seem to make much difference at the time. As far as my behavior and the moral aspects of my character were concerned, the church wasn't even part of my life. My values were much more personal, more practical.

The amazing thing is that I was the kind of leader who led correctly. You know, I used to get onto the guys on the team about swearing and being nasty. I never could be nasty or ignorant to anyone. That wasn't me; I wasn't raised like that. A lot of people look at some of these wild and crazy guys and they believe that's the real sports image today. But what I was saying and doing was really contrary to that.

I was always a pleasant, humble guy until I got on the field. I was never mean or bitter or crazy or anything like that. I didn't do crazy stuff. But I was a tough competitor and I'd do anything legal to whip you, any way I could. There were a few times later in my life when I went to jail, for ignorant reasons. And they really were ignorant reasons, every single time! I can't always say I was entirely innocent, but in every single case it was primarily a case of being in the wrong place at the wrong time, and doing something really ignorant. But I'll come to that a little later.

The first thing that happened when I arrived in Tallahassee was that somebody told me they wanted me and all the other new scholarship athletes to go up for what they called their "Summer Enrichment Program." They said it was like some kind of accelerated academic program to help us get a head start on college. At first I thought that would be exciting, but they told me we'd be staying in these really nice dorms where we'd be living during the rest of the year. But, as it turned out, they lied to me.

I got there and found out they wanted us to stay in some nasty old rooms about the size of a closet, and that really hurt me. One of the main reasons I decided to go to FSU was because of the dorms. When my mother and I came up for the tour, they showed us these really nice rooms where the football players stayed, and I was looking forward to that. But when I saw those dumpy little cells they had for summer students, I called home and told my mother what was going on, and I had tears in my eyes. That really hurt, because they had lied to me and got me up there with false promises.

I remember going to the first class on the first day of summer school and the teacher was late. I sat there for several minutes and I finally said to myself, *Man, this is crazy. What am I doing here?!* So I got up and walked out and never came back. When they came around to get me signed up for some kind of summer program, I said, "No, man, I'm not going to do that, because this is not what you promised me."

So I found a job and I just worked that summer, and that turned out to be the best decision I could have made. I had just gotten out of high school and I wasn't ready to go back to school so soon. I needed some space. I needed to chill a little bit and get used to my new surroundings. The last thing I needed at that time was some drone professor pushing me through some crash academic program in the middle of summer.

Some of my friends who stayed there all summer got so far behind in their studies from making bad grades in those classes that they were never able to catch up. Some of them fell so far behind academically, because of that, that they eventually washed out of school and had to quit football. But I fooled everybody. I just went ahead, got a job, had a great summer, and I got my bearings. When the regular semester started, I got a fresh start like everybody else when they showed for classes in the fall.

After that I got a better dorm room and I got a little better adjusted and acclimated to the campus. I was working out and training, getting ready for the season, and it turned out to be a real blessing. I mean, the job I had was nothing to brag about! I was either cleaning up this old warehouse or driving all over Tallahassee picking up boxes and parts. Since I didn't know my way around very well, I was always getting lost. But if I was having a bad day, I would just go back to my dorm room and wait around for a couple of hours, then I'd get directions from somebody who knew the city better than I did and I'd go on back to my job!

When the season started, Coach Bowden could see that I was serious about the game, and by the end of season I was starting at cornerback. I had played both quarterback and safety in high school, but when I went to college the coaches realized that I would be strongest either at wide receiver or cornerback, and I chose corner because I thought I could become a starter a little sooner at that position. That turned out to be a good choice.

My high school sweetheart joined me at Florida State in my sophomore year, and we dated for about two years while I was there. That was cool. It was fun being with the same girl I'd dated all those years. But she was a Caucasian and she didn't really understand my relationship with my family. High school was one thing, and she never hassled me then, but I think she thought I should have devoted myself to her after we got to FSU, and she expected me to put my family second. But my family came first, before everything. They always have.

She became jealous of my relationships with my sister, my mother, and my aunt. And one day it all came to a head, so I told her I just couldn't take it anymore. My family was going to come before everything else, and whether she left or stayed they were going to be number one with me. So we just broke it off and she went back home to Fort Myers.

It was painful for me because we had been together so long. I came back from practice one day and she was gone. She had moved back home, and it really jarred me at first, but it turned out to be a blessing in the end.

Getting It Done

There's a bad rap on professional athletes that you hear all the time. People say, "These guys have just been given a pass all through life and they've never had to do anything but play ball." That's really unfair, but even if that's true in some cases, it wasn't true for me, because I worked very hard for everything I got. I may have been blessed with talent, but I always worked to make sure I could be the best in every situation. I put a lot more pressure on myself than any of my coaches or teachers ever put on me.

I've been told that they still show my old videotapes to the new guys at Florida State, showing them how I used to practice. They're still doing that to this day. They considered me to be one of the best, but I was never satisfied with that because I always wanted to go one more level, one more step, one more notch. There wasn't anything especially moral or religious in my attitude about it at the time, but I just had a lot of drive, a lot of self-respect, and a lot of self-discipline.

There's a story about me leaving during a baseball game at Florida State, going over to the track meet and running in two events, and then coming back to finish the game before it was over. But that's not the way it happened. It was actually a double-header and after the first game I went over to run in the 4x100 relay in my baseball pants. Then I came back later and played in the next baseball game and got the game-winning run in the Seminoles' second game of the day. But it wasn't as if I had left in the middle of a game or anything like that.

It just so happened that I had major events in all three sports on the same day and I felt like I'd be letting my teams down if I didn't do my best to compete in each of them. I think somebody in the media picked up on that and it all got blown out of proportion, but the important thing was that I always did have a strong work ethic and a sense of loyalty to my teammates.

Nobody had to tell me right from wrong: I could see from my own family background—and particularly from my fathers—that some of what they were doing was wrong, and that gave me a strong sense of self-discipline. While I was still at Florida State I decided I needed to stop using profanity. Everybody knows there's a lot of cursing and swearing around a locker room, but I didn't want to be doing that. I thought it was wrong, so I decided I would stop myself from swearing with a system of behavior modification that I invented for myself. I decided to use the one thing I loved most of all—money!

My Uncle Billy was still selling drugs at that time and he always made sure I had access to money. My aunt worked hard, too, and along with my parents and my other family members who chipped in to help me through college, I usually had plenty of money in my pockets. They kept me with money so I wouldn't have to ask nobody for nothing, and at that time I loved money more than anything else.

My mother was still working two jobs; my stepfather was working, and my biological father was working for the state, so between all of them I had finances, but I also had this bad mouth. When I made up my mind I was going to learn to control my tongue, I came up with this plan. I'd get a hundred dollars in five-dollar bills and keep it in my billfold. Every time I'd lose my temper and swear, or whenever I'd just forget and come out with something nasty, I'd give whoever was standing there a five-dollar bill.

Now, I don't know how much money I gave away before I got the point and broke myself of the habit, but it wasn't long before I stopped using profanity altogether. For a guy who loved money the way I did, the idea of giving it away like that was more than I could take! But that's really just another example of the kind of determination I had.

Whenever I realized I needed to turn a corner and try something new or do something better, I believed I could just set my mind to it and get it done. Most of the time I could. But sometimes I couldn't.

chapter five

CREATING A MONSTER

I didn't have any real anticipation of what might happen at the end of my college career, but I knew that I was probably going to be a first-round draft pick in the NFL, and I knew I wanted to continue with professional baseball as long as I could. My time at Florida State was pretty sensational. I played in four major bowl games during those years, and we won them all. In 1985 we beat Oklahoma State in the Gator Bowl 34 to 23. The next year we defeated Indiana in the All-American Bowl 27 to 13. We beat Nebraska in the Fiesta Bowl in 1988 by a score of 31 to 28, and during my senior year in 1989 we beat Auburn in the Sugar Bowl 13 to 7.

Somewhere in the record books at Doak Campbell Stadium somebody wrote that "Deion Sanders was the finest defensive back in Florida State history." Whether or not that's true, they honored me as such when my jersey was officially retired by the university in 1995. That was something I will always cherish. I also won the Jim Thorpe Award in 1988, and that was another very special honor. That trophy is given to the player chosen as the nation's top defensive back.

Some people say I became a legend at FSU, and if that's true the legend really took off during my junior and senior seasons after I adopted the nickname "Prime Time." But I was always known as one of the hardest-working players on the Florida State team. I worked hard, stayed in good condition, and I studied my playbook religiously. I had 14 career interceptions and ranked second all-time when I left college at the end of the 1988 season.

In baseball, I was a member of the Seminoles' College World Series baseball team, as a center fielder, and I participated in several track and field events as well. I'm also proud of the fact that I still hold the record for the longest interception return for a touchdown, earned when I took one back for 100 yards in the game against Tulsa in my first season.

During those illustrious college days, I was fortunate enough to be named All-American in 1986 by the Sporting News, Associated Press, the Football News, and UPI. The next two years I was named All-American by AP, UPI, the Football Writers Association, the Sporting News, Football News, Walter Camp, Kodak, Scripps Howard, and I was named to the NCAA Concensus All-American First Team two years running.

Making a Name

With all that, it was pretty clear I would turn pro one way or the other when the time came, but there was so much going on that I hardly had time to think about what that would actually mean.

I had already been drafted by the Royals and decided not to play baseball at that time. I had played all sports in high school, so my natural tendency was to play all sports in college, too. But by the end of my sophomore year I realized that was too much for me. Traveling, playing ball, and also trying to keep up my grades was killing me, so I decided to quit baseball and just concentrate on football. But no sooner had I made that decision than I got drafted anyway. This time I was taken by the New York Yankees, and they gave me such a nice signing bonus that I decided I would go pro my junior year in college and play baseball during the off-season.

As soon as I signed on with the Yankees, they sent me down to their farm team, but I went from Single-A to Triple-A in six weeks. That was a blessing, but it meant that when I went back to college I could only play as a walk-on because I had accepted money in the pros. So I let my scholarship at FSU go, but suddenly the sky was the limit because now I had my own money. Agents were helping me out, and I let it be known that I could do anything now because I was a walk-on and not subject to the same restrictions as scholarship players!

The coaches couldn't complain about my expensive suits and shoes and all the jewelry I was flashing because I was a walk-on. I mean, I lived a wonderful life my senior year! I was one of the main guys at Florida State, getting a lot of press and media attention, and I had all that going for me. I was also getting media attention as a professional baseball player, but I felt like somehow or other I needed to take it on up another notch.

I was just sitting in my dorm room one afternoon when somebody came in and handed me a list from some sports magazine that showed all the top players in the National Football League and what they were being paid. I mean, my eyes shot wide open! As I looked down that list, I saw two things. First, I saw that wide receivers, quarterbacks, and running backs were making a lot of money. But, second, I saw that cornerbacks were not making a lot of money!

Literally, that was an eyeopener. I said to myself, *Deion Sanders, you're a cornerback. Cornerbacks don't make much money. But you want to make a lot of money. What are you going to do? Remember what you told your mother? You said, "Mama, I'm gonna be rich one day. I'm gonna make a lot of money and you'll never have to work another day in your life." How you gonna keep that promise to your mama? How you gonna be a cornerback in the NFL and make a whole lot of money?*

So that's where it started. That was the day I started creating the monster. At that moment I decided I had to come up with an image. When I was playing basketball in high school, I had the nickname "Prime Time." My best friend, Richard Fain, gave me that name. I scored something like 36 points in the basketball game one night. I had a few dunks, and I was really on a roll. Richard, who also played baseball and football with me all the way through school, looked at me at one point and said, "Man, you prime time!"

I thought, *Cool! I like that.* So after that everybody started calling me Prime Time. When I got to college my license plate said "DEION," and before long everybody knew that Deion was "Prime Time." So when I was sitting there my sophomore year looking at that list of NFL players, I said, *Man, I gotta create something that's going to make me my money.*

I decided I was going do something with Prime Time. This character, this persona, was going to be much more than just an athlete. He was going to be a total entertainer! So after that I started coming out with these crazy comments and being very outspoken and flashy and flamboyant, with a neck full of jewelry and all that.

I was wearing my do-rag on my head underneath my helmet, and I was serious into jewelry. Before long it was apparent that the new look had separated me from the norm. I remember how big it got because after about a year of that, sometime during my junior year, we had a big press day at Florida State where all the media and fans could come in and meet all the people on the team. Coach Bowden had a sign with his name on it, and when I looked over there I saw this big group lined up to meet him.

That was pretty impressive. But there was also a sign with my name on it and a poster saying, "Prime Time," and the people who wanted to talk to me were lined up over there. And when I looked at my line, there were at least a hundred, maybe a hundred and fifty people, waiting to meet me!

I thought, *Man, this Prime Time stuff is something else!* Because everybody wanted to see this flamboyant, egotistical, arrogant, outspoken young man, and they didn't realize that it was all an act. Prime Time was a character—a caricature of this cocky black football dude that I had created. But the fans and the media were totally captivated by it.

I knew what I was doing, all right, but by nature my personality was really the opposite of what I was creating. Still, I created it, I maximized it, I exploited it, and it came out to be very prosperous. There were times when the act nearly overpowered the actor, because people were always expecting a show. They didn't realize that I was only that way when I was out on the field doing my thing. At home I was somebody else altogether.

But think about it: Michael Jackson has a flamboyant, flashy personality when he's up on stage. But does he wear that glove all the time? No. Of course not. Does Eddie Murphy really go around telling jokes all the time? No way! You hear sports announcers say things like, "Remember folks, this is not war; it's a game; it's entertainment!"

They try to remind people that what we do on the field is just a job, a show, a form of entertainment. But people don't buy that. In fact, I'm not even certain most players buy it. Some of us act like it's a life and death matter, not just a game. But people really need to know the difference, on the field and off.

I got to the point where I had to remind people—including the media sometimes—that it was just a game for me. If they were too serious about my on-the-field routine, then they had been tricked. If the press bought all the stuff I was doing out there as Prime Time, then I had manipulated the heck out of them. In fact, I think that's the main reason so many of them hate me today. They finally realized they were letting themselves be manipulated!

Man to Man

People sometimes think that players and coaches spend a lot of time together in college ball the way they do in a lot of high schools, but that's not the case. Coach Bowden and I spoke mostly in passing during my entire four years in college. Basically, he was an offensive coach, and if you played on the defense you worked primarily with your own defensive coaches, and that's what I did. I didn't need to see the head coach very often.

The only times we really spoke was when I was in trouble, and I remember a couple of times when that happened. The main one was when none of the seniors was attending classes. I had good reason not to attend: I had just gotten a suitcase full of money to go play baseball that summer, which meant that I couldn't be a scholarship player anymore. Since I was a walk-on, I was living in a private condo and driving a brand-new car and doing different stuff.

I knew I was going to be in the top five picks in the draft the next year, and I was already playing for the Yankees farm system. So one thing that definitely was not on my mind was going to classes at Florida State. I wasn't even thinking about graduating, because I got out of college exactly what I went there for. Most of the time I was working out, going through workouts on the practice field, or hanging with my homeys.

I had a problem with things like history and algebra and meteorology and all that stuff I would never need in my entire life. To this day nobody has ever asked me for the logarithm of A-squared plus B-squared or the barometric pressure of anything. Some people need that stuff but I could never see the point. I was never on academic probation or anything like that—I always kept my grades up. But I was busting it every afternoon at practice and I knew that as soon as the season was over I was going to be out of there. I wasn't even going to be back the next spring because I was playing baseball. I wasn't thinking about school; I wasn't going to class, I was doing everything else but going to class. But Coach Bowden had this meeting for seniors, and it was obvious he was there to lay down the law.

He said, "Now, men, this is just ignorant. None of you seniors are going to class and that's not right. Can you tell me who's not going to class?"

I looked around, didn't see anybody raising their hands, so I stuck my hand up and I said, "I ain't. I ain't going!" And I looked around at my teammates and they were all smiling and shaking their heads, but they weren't saying a thing. I wasn't doing that to challenge the coach or to be smart-aleck about it. I was just being honest. So I said, "You know what? You guys are something else. I can't believe you just sit up here and lie like that!"

All the guys on the team looked up to me; they were my boys and we were tight. But the coaches broke us up into our position groups, and the defensive backfield coach got about three of us who weren't going to class and he started going down the line.

He looked at another player—one of my best friends, Alfonso "Alleycat" Williams—and he said, "Cat, no teams are looking at you. You're not going anywhere. How can you not go to college?" And Cat just slid down in his chair and didn't say anything. Then the next guy was this white guy named Stan Shiver, who was an outstanding hitter and one of our best defensive players. Coach said, "Stan, you could possibly get drafted, but you want to do well in college don't you? I can't understand why you're not going to class!"

Then he looked at me and he just shook his head, because he knew I was a leader and he was disappointed with me. But I already had a baseball contract and I wasn't about to go back to class. He said, "All right, just to show you how serious this is, none of you three will be starting on Saturday."

We looked at each other for a couple of seconds and finally I said, "Coach, now let me get this straight. I can understand what you're doing and that you want to make a point and all that, but let me ask you something. What are you gonna tell the kids? What are you gonna tell the fans and the TV audience when I don't start at cornerback? Are you gonna tell them that Prime Time is not playing because he wasn't going to class this week? You gonna tell them I was a bad little boy? You know those kids look up to me, so what you gonna tell those kids?"

I should have majored in psychology. Anyway, I started on Saturday.

The next time I talked to Coach Bowden was after we came back from Christmas break, and this was after I had gotten into a scrape with a security guard down in Fort Myers. I got taken down to jail and it was a big mess. But about the time we all got back to school in January, I got this call from one of the coaches.

They called me while I was over at my girlfriend's apartment and I didn't know what they wanted to talk to me about, but they said, "Deion, Coach Bowden wants to see you in his office, and it's an emergency." So I went over to the coach's office and I was sitting there wondering what in the world he wanted to see me about, and about that time he walked in and said, "Deion Sanders, I'm appalled at you! I can't believe you did this."

After he spelled out what he was talking about, I just looked at him and I said, "First of all, Coach, I wasn't in school when this happened. I was at home on my own time and on my own business. I wasn't at the university, so I didn't do anything at the university, to the university, or for the university. Second of all, that whole deal was a screwup and I didn't do nothing wrong."

Well, Coach Bowden didn't like my attitude, so he said, "Okay, I hear that. But I don't think I'm going to let you play in the Sugar Bowl."

"Not let me play?" I said. "Okay. That's cool. Bless you. I'll see you later." And I just got up, left the room, and slammed the door on my way out.

I went straight home and went to bed. Well, I wasn't there very long before the phone started ringing and somebody said, "Deion, they want to see you!" I honestly didn't care if I played in the Sugar Bowl or not. If Coach didn't want to play me, that was his business and it was fine by me either way. Regardless whether I played or not, I was going in the draft and I was going be playing in the NFL the following year. But, sure enough, my position coach called me back and said, "Get ready, Sanders. You're going to the Sugar Bowl."

Despite incidents like that, I can honestly say that I have the utmost respect for Coach Bobby Bowden, because he was an outstanding coach, a wonderful man, and he let me do my thing. I doubt if any other player has ever had the range of self-expression or the personal freedom that I enjoyed on that team. It didn't have anything to do with sports—the things he let me do, the things I said in the media, or the things I did to build myself up, to glorify myself, and to make the kind of money I wanted to make. But he let me go.

He knew that on the field I was playing hard and doing a good job. I was setting an example for young people. He also knew I wasn't a bad kid. I had played baseball that summer, but because of my popularity with the younger kids I had so much power that it would have been difficult to try to rein me in.

I used to keep $5,000 on me at all times. I had a drop-top LeBaron with a cell phone. Remember now, this was 1988, so that was pretty hot back then. I mean, I was "the man" on campus. And I used to take care of all my teammates. They'd say, "Prime, let me hold something, brother," and I'd give them $100 and let them go eat at a nice place. I used to take care of them. I'd say, "What you need, man? Here you go. Here, go buy you some sweatsuits or some sport shoes or whatever you need, man." I took care of my boys.

I had enough power on that team that when there were problems, they brought them right to me. And I'd sit down in my room and hold counseling sessions, and when I'd tell them what they needed to do, they listened, and they did it.

That was power. I know that Coach Bowden realized that too much power in the hands of the wrong people, especially if they were leading them in the wrong direction, could be a disaster. He would have stopped me if he thought that was the right thing to do. But, fortunately, even though I wasn't a Christian at that time and I didn't have any particular religious outlook, I was leading people more or less in the right direction.

I did hear, however, that the year after I left Coach Bowden called a team meeting and he said, "Fellows, Deion Sanders is gone. There ain't gonna be no more of all that stuff around here. From now on your primary responsibility is to this university, to me, to the coaching staff, and to your teammates, and that's how it's going to be." But in all fairness to Coach Bowden, he let me be who I was. I think it was good for the team at that time, and it was definitely a blessing for me. So I'm grateful to him for that, for his patience, and for his understanding.

I'll Take Both!

By my senior year at Florida State, I was having enormous success. I had already been playing baseball for the Yankees and I was back on campus for my final year of college football. I hadn't really made up my mind whether I was going to be a baseball or football player in the pros, so I finally decided I wasn't going to decide. Why should I decide? I grew up playing two sports—actually three sports—so I said, *Why can't I just keep on doing what I've been doing? Why settle for one or the other when I can have both?!*

When it came time for the NFL draft in the spring of my senior year, I was taken in the first round by Atlanta. The fact of the matter is, I ended up going to Atlanta because I told all the other teams that called my agent that Atlanta was where I wanted to play. That was 1989, and Dallas had the first pick that year. Green Bay was second, Detroit was third, Kansas City was fourth, and Atlanta was fifth.

I knew I wasn't going to Dallas because they were desperate for a quarterback and it was pretty obvious they were going to take Troy Aikman, who had just finished at UCLA that year. So I told all the other teams, "Do not draft me! I'm playing baseball." Detroit was making moves like they were going to do it anyway and I told their scouts that if they drafted me I would demand so much money they would have to put me on lay-away. In fact, I wanted to go to Atlanta. Atlanta was a two-sport town, and it was a city with a large black population, and I thought the fans in Georgia would understand me better than some of the other places I could have gone.

I didn't want to go to some city where I would have been miserable, because I knew I would be misunderstood in most places. But really, Atlanta and I chose each other, and it was a wonderful relationship for the first four years I was there. It was tough to leave Atlanta, especially playing two sports there. I remember the media interviewing people when I left the city and they were all upset. When I go back now people still talk about the things I did when I was there. That was a time I will never forget.

I was living the kind of life I had only dreamed of up to that time. I was finally building my mother that million-dollar dream home I had promised her, and that became the main priority of my first year in the pros.

I was just spending money, getting whatever I wanted to get, and doing whatever I wanted to do. Growing up the way I did I didn't see anybody but drug dealers that had very much money. I never saw much jewelry unless it was drug dealers wearing it. I never saw anything like that until I started getting over to the other side of town during high school. I always wanted to have nice things, and I always wanted to be able to do something special for my mother, so finally being able to do all that was really a dream come true.

If you've never had much money and you suddenly get a lot of money, there are all sorts of new temptations and problems to deal with. But fortunately I had good people around me, and I never let the money have me. I always knew I had the money. To this day, I still have the same attorney that I had at the beginning, Eugene Parker, and he's a dear friend. Eugene has always been the steady hand to help me through the tough times.

Long before I became a Christian, Eugene was there. He's been a devout Christian since day one, since I first met him. He wasn't one of the guys that tried to push me, but I viewed his lifestyle and I knew he was okay. He was good people. Eugene never stepped out of line. I never heard this man curse, never saw him get upset. He was and is a devoted family man and he loves the Lord. But he's been that way since I've known him.

One thing some people find a little strange is that the very first professional football game I ever attended was the first one I played in, and I scored a touchdown in it. That's the week I scored a touchdown for the Falcons and hit a home run for the Yankees, so that was a special time for me, too.

I wasn't even aware what I had done until the media started blowing it up. I had hit a home run before I left the Yankees, and then I showed up in Atlanta for my first game as a Falcon at the end of that week, so I was just doing my thing. But the press really made a big deal out of it. A home run and a touchdown in two professional sports in the same week!

Lots of press. Lots of clips. But it's funny that the things I've accomplished have never been all that big a deal to me personally. Never have. But the accomplishments have been nice and maybe they help set some sort of standard for other young guys to shoot for. Like being the only player to play in the World Series and the Super Bowl in the same season. That doesn't happen very often, but it's cool to know I could do that.

I was with the Falcons five years before I finally moved on. Then I went to San Francisco. I only played there one season, but it was a glorious year. In many ways it was the most spectacular year of my athletic career, but it's also the season that the Lord started calling me.

chapter six

GROWING PAINS

The most difficult part of my life growing up was knowing that my father was just around the corner and he wasn't there for me when I needed him. Part of that was hearing my mother and other people saying things about my father and, little by little, coming to believe that my father had no interest in me and no love for his son. He did try at times to seem more like a father to me, but it was so hard for me to talk to him easily and openly, or even to ask him for presents at Christmastime. I remember those as some of the most difficult times of my life.

I still carry the memories. People don't realize how impressionable their children are. But they see; they remember. I have vivid memories from the time when I was six or seven years old, seeing my mother and father arguing and fighting with each other. They were difficult times. I trusted my mother—she had always been there for me—but I wasn't sure who was right and who was wrong whenever they would argue. I was still trying to sort that out. I know I just wanted them to stop it and be nice to one another.

The second most difficult thing, I think, was dealing with all the negativity from other people. I knew that I had a lot to do with it because of the image I created. But so many of those people who made judgments about me never really knew me.

When you have a visible platform as a successful athlete, whether it's in school, college, or later in the pros, people—and especially reporters and sportswriters—take a lot of liberties in the things they say about you and the way they write about you. Most of the time they act as if our own feelings and emotions have no importance at all. And even when I tried to ignore the things they say—as I do now and have always tried to do—their words could still be very hurtful. Some people just seem to take pleasure in wounding athletes and other people in the public eye. But it wouldn't bother me so much if it didn't affect the people around me. My family in particular.

I don't care about all that today as much as I used to. But when I was growing up and when I was just getting started as a professional athlete, there were people who said some things that were very painful for me. And it was very painful for my parents. It really bothered them, especially toward the end of my college career when people were saying some awful things about me in the national media.

Taking Advantage

Along with comments, slurs, and criticisms of various kinds, I've also had to face some racial stuff over the years. My success on the field probably helped defuse some of that, but nothing can get rid of all of it. I have to jump ahead of my story a little bit to do this, but to put things in perspective, I think it's important to relate some of the incidents that show the kinds of things I had to deal with in those days. These were things that really happened, and in a couple of cases I had to go to jail over what I feel were black/white issues.

The first was when I was a senior in college and I had gone home for Christmas. I was at one of the big department stores in the local mall in Fort Myers, buying some twenty-dollar earrings for my stepsister. The saleslady got the earrings out of the glass case and I gave her a twenty-dollar bill and she turned around toward the cash register.

The store was packed, and on the way over she got into a conversation with another clerk, but as she was walking I did a little mental arithmetic and realized that with tax the total would be a little over $20. So I went over and said, "Ma'am, here's another five to go with the twenty I just gave you."

She looked at me like I was a creature from another planet, and she said, "You didn't give me any money."

I thought, *Oh, brother! Here we go.* And I said, "Yes, ma'am, I sure did."

But she insisted, even louder than before, "You did not give me any money!"

I just shook my head and looked over at my friend who was standing there.

Finally, I said, "Yes, ma'am, I did!" My lifelong friend Richard Fain had come with me and he had been standing there beside me the whole time. So I said, "Look, lady, my friend was standing right there and he can vouch for the fact that I gave you a twenty-dollar bill."

She didn't like my tone one bit, so she called me the N-word and accused me of lying, and that did it. I reached over the counter and grabbed her arm and said, "Look here, lady. You listen to me. I gave you a twenty-dollar bill and then another five dollars for the tax, so you don't need to go calling me any names!"

By this time some big guy saw what was happening and came running from across the store, trying to be the hero. But I saw him out of the corner of my eye and when he came up and started to grab me, I wheeled around and cold-cocked him and he just hit the floor.

Now all of a sudden we had everybody's attention. The whole store was catching this action and it was starting to look pretty ugly. So I said to my friend, who was standing there wide-eyed, with his mouth just hanging open, "Man, this is crazy! Let's go find a phone. There's going to be trouble here." So we went out into the mall to a pay phone to call home.

When my stepfather answered the phone, I told him, "Will, I'm just calling to let you know I might get into something down here. I might get into a little trouble because I had to hit this dude down at the mall."

I had played ball in this town my whole life and you would think somebody might have recognized me and said something in my defense. But while I was standing there explaining things to my stepfather on the phone, one of the security guards from the mall came running up to me and said, "Okay, you, come on! You're coming with me."

I looked back at him and said, "Okay, just a minute, I'm talking to my stepfather."

But he wasn't hearing that. He reached around me and pushed down the button on the phone and grabbed the receiver out of my hand.

I said, "Hey, man, there's a way to do things, you know! You don't have to go acting like that!"

But I just shook my head and went with him because I knew there would be questions and forms to fill out and stuff like that. As we were walking down the hall I could see this local policeman approaching in a big hurry and, oh man, now he wanted to be the tough guy! So this cop came up and grabbed me by the arm and tried to show out in front of the other police officers.

They were pushing me along and by this time two or three others had come and they started pushing and shoving me down the hall, and finally they took me down one of these little tunnels that they have in the mall and they stopped right on the other side of the door.

I just looked at them and said, "Man, what's going on here?"

I had on some chains, a couple of rings, and I was flashing a little gold that day. They didn't know who I was or where I was from, and I guess I must have looked like a drug dealer to them. Even though my picture had been in all the newspapers and I had played football on TV for years, it was obvious they didn't know me from the King of Spain. But with all the jewelry I was wearing, they decided they had a live one on their hands!

It wasn't looking too good for me, or Richard either, with a half dozen cops about ready to break my neck. So as soon as we stepped out into the hallway, I grabbed hold of the door and said, "Hey, man, can my friend come with me?"

At that exact instant they grabbed me, threw me up against the concrete wall, and started punching me and roughing me up. Now, I was in pretty good shape, an athlete, practically a pro by this time, so I reached out and shoved one of those guys away from me and tried to make a break for the door.

My friend, seeing all this, yelled out, "Hey, man, leave him alone! He didn't do anything!" Now Richard was the guy who gave me the nickname "Prime Time," so he was always looking out for me. He was with me, but I wasn't planning on waiting for any courtesy calls. I started to run and just as I broke for the door, I heard the police officer yell out, "Shoot him!" And I just froze in my tracks!

They came running after me, shoved me outside the doors and into the parking lot behind one of the buildings, and this time they really started pounding on me. One guy was pushing my face up against this big green Dumpster, and a bunch of young kids who saw all the commotion started gathering around to see what was up, and when they recognized me several of them started screaming and yelling. "It's Deion Sanders! It's Deion Sanders!"

So I said to the cops, "Come on, man! Don't do this stuff in front of the kids! Can't you see that they're seeing all this?" The kids were all yelling and screaming my name because they knew who I was. But the cops didn't know from nothing, and they handcuffed me, shoved me in the police car, and drove me down to the station.

I honestly thought they were going to break my arms, shoving handcuffs on me and pulling my arms up behind my back. But when we got down to the police station, one of the officers who opened the car door took one look at me and he said, "Oh my God, it's Deion Sanders!"

The chief of police was the father of one of the kids I grew up with and he knew I wasn't a thief or a drug dealer, so he yelled, "Get the cuffs off him!" And they took the cuffs off me and I went into the station. I explained to the duty officer what had really happened down there, and I wrote it all up and they realized that I was telling the truth. But, unfortunately, I guess that didn't satisfy everybody.

When I pushed the guy up against the wall and started to run, nothing was wrong with him. He may have been embarrassed, and his pride might have been wounded, but he wasn't hurt physically in any way. But as soon as he found out who I was, he sued me. I still didn't have any money at the time, but that didn't stop him. He made a case of it and my lawyers advised me to just settle out of court. This rent-a-cop claimed he was injured and couldn't work, but I think he just saw a chance to take advantage of a situation and he didn't care that I was innocent from the start.

Easy Money

That's one incident that really bothered me. Another one happened when I went down to play Triple-A baseball in Richmond, Virginia. I was playing for the Yankees and we were playing the Richmond Braves, and the local fans were really giving us a hard time and they were harassing both me and Carolyn, who was my fiancée at the time. Of course, they were doing that to get to me. I was having a terrible game anyway, and finally they took me out of the game, so I got dressed and went on up into the stands to get her and said, "Come on, Baby, let's go. Let's go on to the hotel."

But the main guy who was giving us a hard time made some racial remark and we locked up with one another, but about the time I grabbed him I said to myself, "No, man, it's not worth it." So I pushed him off, took Carolyn by the arm, and we left and went back to the hotel. But as I was sitting there in my room, there was a knock on the door and when I opened it there was a policeman standing there. So I said, "Yes, sir, what can I do for you?"

He said, "Mr. Sanders, will you come with us, please? You're under arrest." I said, "For what?" And he said, "Harassment, assault and battery, and he listed a half dozen things that just blew me away. So we went down to the police station, and as we were going inside I saw the guys who had been taunting us and they had torn and ripped their shirts so it would look like I had abused them.

It was so funny, and the magistrate was a good ol' boy and he gave me something like a $5,000 bond—something crazy like that. Now stuff like that is major news for an athlete and makes you look bad all over the country. And, once again, I ended up settling out of court, paying the guys off, and also being required to build some sort of plaque in their ballpark to benefit some charity.

It was absolutely stupid, and what infuriates me was that the law wasn't interested in my side of the story; they were much more inclined to believe these dishonest citizens who made a claim against me. They all just saw it as a way to pick up a few bucks, and I've always felt that these things, and others like them over the years, were largely racially motivated.

The next time I almost went to jail was in my hometown of Fort Myers. I was with the same guy, my good friend Richard Fain, and we were in the car coming from my home. I had moved my mother out to Gateway, which is a wonderful community close to the airport. We were riding down with the top dropped back. Benz, big black Mercedes, looking good, me and him, young boys, ball caps turned around backward, you know, music bumping. And we saw this police officer coming off the highway.

We looked at him, he looked at us, and he came up right behind us. Traffic was real slow and we couldn't go anywhere, but in a couple of minutes the lights come on and he pulled us over.

I said, "What's all this about? Why are you pulling us over?"

He just started writing out a ticket for following a car too closely. I was so hot I just left the car and walked all the way home. That was the only thing I could do to cool down. And that was in my own hometown!

But I think the basis of my trouble, in all these things, was that I've always done things my way. But those are things where I got in trouble and where I either went to jail or was threatened with jail over some nonsense.

There's one other racism story, and this one is just ridiculous. I was in Cincinnati playing baseball a few years back. When I'm just getting around the ballpark or coming and going to the field during the season, a lot of the times I'll use my little Honda Helix scooter. When I was in Cincinnati, I lived right downtown and just a couple of miles from the ballpark, so it was convenient to just drive there in my cart.

One day I had come in for a game—we were playing the Braves that night and I had just joined the team, traded over to Cincinnati. So I asked the clubhouse guys, "What's the quickest way for me to get out of here? There are a lot of fans out there and I'm on my little scooter, so is there some kind of shortcut or some back way I can get out quicker?"

One guy said, "Sure, Deion, I know a good way." And he told me a way that I'd never been before. I had parked my scooter down in the tunnel, so I went down there and I headed back up the tunnel, and this guy showed me which door to take. But, as always, there was this security guard who had another idea. As I was driving along I saw that there was a high curb at one place and there was just no way I could get my scooter over that without tearing it up completely. So I just turned around and headed back when I heard some guy yelling at me, "Hey, get out of here! Hey, you, get out of here! You know you can't go that way!"

So I said, "Okay, man. I'm just leaving. You don't need to yell at me. I'll go."

But that didn't satisfy him. He started yelling even louder, "Hey, get out of here!"

So I said, "Sir, there's a way to handle people, and that ain't it!" I'm sure he didn't realize I was a player. I was in shorts and had my hat down. Besides, I was new on the team and I was on a scooter and he wasn't expecting any of that. He just thought I was an employee or a custodian I suppose.

Anyway, he was this older white guy and he was really giving me some lip, so I said, "Look, man, that's no way to talk to anybody!" And he reached out and grabbed me by the shoulder and said, "I'll take you to jail, boy!" and he tried to pull me off my scooter. Well, I didn't need any of that stuff, so I just gave it the gas and took off. I thought, *Man, just let me on out of here! This dude is crazy.*

But this old guy was running along behind me, trying to grab hold of me, and he stumbled and fell. So I rode all the way back around the tunnel, parked under the clubhouse, and went back inside and said, "Your security guard just came unglued down there! He was yelling at me and trying to pull me off my scooter, and he fell down while he was chasing me. I know he's going to be upset, so you better go check on him."

Knowing these things have a way of turning ugly, I called my attorney right away and let him know what was going on, but it wasn't twenty minutes before the police showed up and told me I was under arrest.

This all happened inside the tunnel and the ballpark, and I'm a player for this team! I mean, it was the night before my birthday and I'm up there sitting for at least 45 minutes and waiting for the police to make up their minds what they were going to do with me. Finally, they all got their heads together and came up with a plan, then they took me down to the station, asked me for all kinds of autographs, and I'm signing all this mess.

Then the next day, on my birthday, I happened to see this guy on the news in a wheelchair with a neck brace and bruises all over his face saying that I dragged him fifty feet through the tunnel. He said I ran over him and cursed him out and that I called him all sorts of names. I couldn't even believe what I was hearing.

Well, in the end we had to go to court and there was this big court trial and the newspapers were full of it for the longest time. But the good news is that I was telling the truth and the court believed my story. I successfully defended my case against this white security officer who had been on the staff for twenty-something years, and who was trying to sue me for a million-something dollars. I won the case, and they threw his claim out of court.

But within days the guy came back and filed a civil suit. He wasn't going to give up without a fight, so I had to go back through the whole process all over again. And I beat him again, on every count, because he was just flat lying and trying to take advantage of the situation.

I'm convinced that in each of these cases, it's either racism, plain and simple, or at the least it's racism tainted by greed and a touch of larceny.

Thank the Lord I had a good attorney. But if that kind of thing is happening to me—a well-known athlete—then I can just imagine that it's happening to lots of other people who may not be as wellknown as I am.

PART II

chapter seven

SOMETHING TO PROVE

Prime Time" was my own creation. I created him while I was still in college. I didn't start out to make a monster, even though in some ways that's what I became. The personality and attitudes I portrayed in that role were only tools to get me a little attention and help me make a name for myself. But before long I was generally thought of by most people as this arrogant young athlete with a proud superstar personality. Part of it was me, of course; but part of it was the media hitting on that made-up image.

Sportswriters weren't just reporting on me, they were giving their personal opinions, using me for a launching pad. And a lot of the time they were just savaging me in the newspapers for the fun of it. Sometimes I'd think I could trust a writer and start telling him the truth, then he would turn around and kill me in the paper the next day.

I remember one time when they brought in this hotshot reporter from ESPN—the all-sports television network—and he came to my home to do a personal interview with me. I mean, the producers had it all set up and they were very cordial and gracious. They said it was going to be some sort of celebrity profile, but it didn't take very long for me to realize that this guy had something else in mind.

In fact, he came there to bury me. But when I saw where he was going and where all his questions were leading, I laid it down to him. I told him the truth, plain and simple. But since they weren't after the truth in the first place — what they were after was sensationalism and higher ratings — they never aired the interview, and that's probably the best thing that could have happened.

The same kind of thing happened later in San Francisco. One of the popular network sports analysts — a guy whose face you've seen in your living room hundreds of times no doubt — came over to my home to tape an interview, and, again, I think they wanted to do a number on me. But I gave them something very different from what they were looking for and, as a result, they never aired the piece. They wanted to make me out to be a villain but they got something totally different and I think that spoiled their plans.

A professional athlete's life is hard enough without taking that kind of beating from the media, but I think the public needs to know the way they come after us sometimes.

The Water Deal

The most sensational spat in my sports career happened when I was having this war of words with a media guy named Tim McCarver back in 1993. I was still playing for the Atlanta Braves, and there was a lot of misunderstanding and miscommunication about the incident at the time. But it made all the papers and the sports talk shows for a long time.

Ever since the 1990 season, I had been playing for the Braves in baseball and the Falcons in football. My contract with the Braves went from the beginning of baseball season to the first of July, when I would start getting ready for football season. So even though the baseball team was still playing, and even though I would frequently come out to practice and suit up just in case they needed me, I wasn't actually under contract. If I played, they would pay me; but if I couldn't make it or if they didn't play me that particular game, then I didn't get paid.

Officially, my contract was up after the first of July. But there were dozens of times when I would fly wherever they were playing so I could be there during the game to pinch-run for them or do whatever I could to help the team. I thought that would be especially helpful during play-offs.

But on this one particular occasion, the Falcons were playing the Miami Dolphins and the Braves were already in the play-offs, matched up against the Pittsburgh Pirates and playing at Three-Rivers Stadium up in Pittsburgh. I wasn't starting for the Braves, of course. I was sitting on the bench for nine innings most of the time, just hoping they might let me pinch-run or -hit for somebody late in the game, but I could see that they had no intention of using me.

At one point I remember thinking, *Why should I just sit there on the bench for nine innings hoping they might let me hit or run for somebody when my secondary back in Atlanta is about to go out on the football field against the Miami Dolphins and Dan Marino, one of the greatest quarterbacks in the game?* The football game started at one o'clock and the baseball game didn't start until 7:30, so, I figured if I took a private plane I'd have plenty of time to make it to both games. So I said, *Okay, if I go down to Atlanta now, I can do my job for the Falcons and still get back here in plenty of time for the Pirates game.* And that's what I did.

But what did the media say? "Oh, yeah, Prime Time's trying to make a name for himself, playing in two professional sports on the same day!" But I wasn't even thinking about that. It never entered my mind until they pointed it out! But I did feel a sense of duty and concern for my teammates. I wanted them to do well and I didn't want to let them down if there was even a chance I might be able to get into the game and help out.

But the general manager of the Braves just blew me up, and then one of the booth announcers tore into me, and he let me have it the whole game, talking about how ignorant and selfish I was. I think "nasty and conceited" were about the nicest things he said about me that day; and I remember going back to the locker room and I was just totally crushed by all the trash they were talking. I wanted to be there to help my team and it seemed like everybody just assumed I was only in it for myself.

When I walked onto the bus after the game, the whole team stood up and cheered and clapped for me because they knew what I was going through and they had heard all the junk on the loudspeakers. But I just went and sat down on the backseat with tears running down my cheeks, and I said, "Thanks, guys. I really needed that." We went out there and played a great game. We lost, but it was a good game and I wanted to be there to help my teammates if they needed me.

Shortly after that we helicoptered over to the airport and flew back to Pittsburgh, sore, hurting both physically and mentally, and I arrived at the stadium before the game started. And it was like the same thing that happened in Atlanta was going to happen all over again in Pittsburgh. They ripped me, insulted me, and tore me apart piece by piece. To this day I don't remember whether we won or lost the baseball game, I was taking so much heat. I was the last guy sitting on the bench, and they could have played me, but it was clear that they weren't going to let me in the game if hell froze over.

Going back and feeling all that pain and all that hurt inside, was just too much for anybody. And this broadcaster named Tim McCarver obviously felt it was his personal duty to rip me totally apart. I said some things at the time, but basically I wanted to let it pass, and the team went on and had a terrific season. We just kept winning all the way through the play-offs. It was really exciting when we finally won the National League pennant and realized we were going to the World Series. That was really big, and after that last big win, everybody just went totally crazy.

In the locker room after the game all the players were throwing champagne and yelling and carrying on like little kids. I never believed in drinking, so I wasn't going to start spraying anybody with champagne like some of the other players were doing, but I grabbed a big bucket and filled it up and I started tossing water around on all the guys. About that time, this broadcast announcer who had been giving me such a hard time all season long came down to the locker room to do his post-game interviews.

Well, there was no particular malice in it, but just to show what a forgiving, easy-going, fun-loving sort of guy I was, I turned and doused this guy with a bucket of water the same way I'd been doing everybody else! I mean, I didn't want him to feel left out since he was so interested in my career! But he was outraged and started yelling that I had assaulted him. The players just laughed and some of the reporters standing around started laughing. But then the media types all ran out and made this big story about me getting even with Tim McCarver, throwing water on him.

By the time McCarver got his story together, I had thrown not just a bucket of water, but ice water all over him! Well, the media had a field day with that, but I never harbored any ill will toward McCarver or anybody else. I won't deny that my feelings had been hurt and I was irritated by all the things he said about me, but I certainly wasn't out to hurt anybody. I felt that McCarver and some of his media pals did me a real disservice.

Part of the problems was that the general manager never told the fans or anybody else that my contract only ran up to July, and that I was coming to the games out of the goodness of my heart. The team manager, Bobby Cox, came to me one day and said, that he wasn't really aware of all the details of my situation and he was sorry about what happened. They never let the fans know that either. But I was going up there because I loved the game and I wanted to do whatever I could—contract or not— to help our guys win.

The Best of Times

Sometimes you have to just stand back and look at things objectively to appreciate the big picture. Getting into the NFL, finally getting that first big contract signed, and then knowing that not only are you playing a game that you love, but you're going to be financially secure, it's just awesome. What a great feeling!

The first thought that ran through my mind when I turned pro was that now my mother could quit her job! And I realized that at last I was finally able to keep my promise to her. She would never have to work another day in her life. When they started breaking ground for her dream house, and when the construction finally got under way, I mean, man, those were the best of times!

But, to be honest, I still remember some of the best times in my life as being those that happened at 1625 Henderson, in Fort Myers, Florida, where I grew up. I mean, we had rats, roaches, and old cars, but we had some good times. It was just like the TV series *Good Times*. We had good times in that house, but when you move up and start doing better—to whom much is given much is required!—suddenly people come after you. They start coming out of the woodwork.

People start reaching at you for money—digging, grabbing at you. They were attacking my mother and my stepfather, hitting them up for money, trying to use them and play on their emotions. It's like there comes a time when you have to make a break with the past. So we couldn't stay down on Henderson Street once I started coming up. But when they finally moved out of that old house down there, we left part of us behind, and we took a lot of good memories with us. But we knew that changes had to come.

I remember going home one last time, to the old house, just after I first got into the NFL. They hadn't finished building my mother's new house yet, and I went down to see my old room and I remember sitting there on the dresser, and I could hear rats scratching inside in the walls and the cabinets like Herbie Hancock! I wanted to spend the night there, but I thought, *Man, I can't sleep like this!* By that time I already had a nice home in Atlanta and my mother's new house was just barely under construction, but I remember being so upset that things were taking so long while my mother and my family were living in those conditions.

As if I needed any more incentive, things like that just drove me to make as much money as I could so my family and I would never again have to live that way. I remember sitting on that dresser and I was just furious that my mother had to be in that situation. I was so upset I couldn't sleep a wink. I didn't leave and go to a hotel or anything like that, but I stayed up all night and I caught the first flight back to Atlanta in the morning.

Earlier when I was telling about what made me run fast as a little kid, I guess I could have said that living in those conditions made me run fast, too. As much as anything else, I wanted to be an outstanding player on the field so that I could make just as much money as possible. I felt like everything depended on me, and I knew that if I didn't make it, and if my mother and stepfather had to go on living in those circumstances, it would be because I had failed to fulfill my promise to my mother.

Did the pressures of wanting to build a better life for myself and my family ever get to be too much? Sure. At times. Especially in baseball, because I'm not on quite the same level as a baseball player that I am as a football player. But I remember thinking, *Man, I just can't take this all the time. Every time I go on the field, the fans are expecting a miracle out of me. I'm trying to live up to their dreams and it's hard enough just living up to my own!*

Football, on the other hand, was always more natural for me, while baseball was more of a challenge. Actually, I think that's probably the main reason I decided to go ahead and pursue baseball as a career, because it was such a challenge. Baseball was a sport that always demanded that I dig down a little deeper and come up with something. I had to focus my concentration and my desire in a way that I never had to do in football. Consequently, the standards that other people set for me in baseball—apart from my own standards—often got me upset.

I always knew that if I was patient, if I played and practiced hard, and if everyone would just leave me alone, I could be the player everybody was talking about. But there were always just too many announcers, reporters, and fans who took pleasure in putting pressure on me and forcing me to play at a higher level. I'd hear things like, "He could be such a great athlete if he'd just settle down and play one sport." Or, "He's just not the athlete he could be if he'd concentrate more." And I would say, "Man, how do you know!? You've never played either sport!"

Simple Gifts

My wife and kids became very important to me through all of that—my daughter in particular. Deiondra had been born in April of 1990, and when she was born suddenly I got a whole new outlook on women. She was so sweet and adorable, and when I would look at her in all her sweet little girl innocence, I began to see women in a new way. I think she helped fill a very special spot in my life.

Then when my son, Deion Luwynn, Jr., came along, he filled a spot that had been empty since my father, Daddy Buck, passed away in 1993. When my son came, I knew that God was going to bless me. We didn't have to check to see whether it was going to be a boy or a girl, I already knew that God had put that little boy in my life because that's what I needed most at that time. Losing my father was painful for me, so when my son came along in December of 1993, it was a gift from God. It was just at the right time.

It's funny because, you know, I'm a strong man. I never show my weakness to anyone. But coming home to see the birth of my daughter was one of the most dramatic and moving experiences of my life. I almost fainted! When Carloyn told me the baby was about to come, I went to the bathroom and splashed water on my face. A few minutes later when I came out somebody said, "Somebody better grab Carolyn; she's about to faint!" And I said, "Yeah, and somebody better grab me, too, because I'm about to faint!"

But having your firstborn child is a very special moment. When Deiondra was born and the nurses got her all cleaned up, I put a little gold necklace around her neck with little gold hearts on it, each one inset with diamonds. And then I had a limo pick us up at the front door of the hospital and drive us all home together, because I wanted my daughter's first ride to be in a limousine.

That was so great. And then a few years later, when my son came, it felt so good. It's nice to have both a boy and a girl, but I'm glad my first-born was my daughter, because I think that softened me and prepared me for being a father. Having that little girl has changed me. It has changed the way I think about women, and about other people in general. I say, "I don't want anybody getting out of line with my daughter, so I shouldn't be messing around with anybody else's little girl!"

Family is important to me now, but so many men in this country haven't made that discovery. Lot of kids these days are growing up in homes without fathers or with fathers who aren't reliable, and they develop the atti-tude that men aren't reliable. They decide that fathers are not to be trusted. I can only say that despite the fact that my own fathers were involved in things they shouldn't have been, I always had a few good influences who helped me develop a sense of personal responsibility.

Now that I've been through some major changes in my life, I realize that it's very hard for people who grow up without a father they can count on to trust in the Lord. If their earthly father let them down, then they have a hard time believing that their heavenly Father will do any better. So that's another reason I want to be trustworthy, reliable, and honest. I want people to see that a man can be a friend, and he can feel love and give love without expecting something in return.

I grew up in a home where I knew I was loved but I never heard the words "I love you." I grew up in a home where I knew my mother worked her tail off for me and she gave me everything. She sacrificed for me. She wore those old no-name jeans so I could wear "Guess?" And she wore those Kmart sneakers so I could wear Nikes. But even though I knew she loved me, she never said it. That just seemed to be something nobody was ever able to do around our house.

Losing the influence of my biological father at such an early age was tough, and then when he died just a few years ago I really struggled because I realized it was too late. I couldn't do anything to make up for all the years we lost. But what hurt me most was realizing that in all those years we had never said "I love you." We knew we loved each other. We understood it. But we never said it. That's why I tell my kids today—a hundred times a day—"Baby, I love you! I think you're great!"

I want them to know how I feel about them. I want them to know they're special, and I preach it everywhere I go. Do you want your kids to have peace in their lives? Do you want them to be dependable and happy, and to radiate self-confidence? Then why don't you tell them how you feel about them? Hold them, hug them, touch them, and say, "Baby, I love you," until they understand how much you really care.

You don't want to wake up one day like I did, losing somebody you loved so much and knowing that you'll never see them again. And knowing that they went to their grave without ever hearing you say, "I love you." When my fathers died, I really struggled with that. Thinking about what I had lost just killed me. I felt as if I had lost a piece of my heart. But because of that experience, I've learned to take the time now and say "I love you" whenever I have the chance.

chapter eight

DYING FOR A CHANGE

When I made my big move in from Atlanta to play for the San Francisco 49ers during the 1994 season, I was running, desperate for a change, and desperately in need of a new challenge. Everybody needs a challenge now and then, but athletes need them more than anybody, and I thrived on it. I needed the adrenaline rush that came from knowing I could play my game, my way, and most of the time be recognized as somebody who could make a difference on the field.

The problem was that the more I accomplished, and the higher I rose in football and baseball, the harder it was to find challenges that were big enough for me. That was my situation. If you've done a lot of things that get you a lot of media attention, as I always have, then you've got to keep pushing. You're looking for newer and bigger challenges to get you pumped. I've always been the kind of athlete that thrives on achievement, high excitement, big games, big plays. I'm the guy who's always trying to improve on his last success. But that was my problem.

The media and the fans kept saying I was good, so that wasn't my problem. Actually, more than good—they said I was outstanding—but all the public acclaim didn't give me any rest. It only meant that I had to keep pushing a little harder all the time to see how good I could really be. But while all this was going through my head, I had these nagging questions: Was it a fact? Was I really all that? Was I that good, or was it just hype?

Talk show guys would say things like, "When Deion Sanders is on the field the magic starts to happen." I mean, there was all kinds of hype like that going around. I had the skills and I knew it, but there was this voice that kept pushing me, saying, "Okay, Prime, show your stuff, man. Show 'em what you're made of!"

But then I would think about where all I had been. I had been an outstanding athlete all my life, growing up playing sandlot ball, making a name in the Pee Wee leagues and Pop Warner ball. You name it. In my junior year at Tallahassee, the Yankees had come to town to sign me up, and the scouts said that if I signed to go professional I could play baseball with the Yankees, make a lot of money, and still play college ball during my final year at Florida State.

They offered me such a nice contract and signing bonus, I accepted, and that was the beginning of my professional career. But from then on I lost my scholarship status at FSU. I continued to play baseball, football, and run track in school, but according to NCAA rules paid professionals can only participate as walk-ons. But since I had my own money, I was doing just fine, and that was okay with me.

Then at the end of my senior year in 1989, I was taken in the first round of the NFL draft by the Atlanta Falcons. I signed with them on September 7, played my first game against the L.A. Rams three days later, and announced my presence by returning my first career interception for 68 yards and a touchdown.

That was cool because just five days before that I had hit a home run for the Yankees in a World Series game, so the touchdown for Atlanta made me the only athlete in modern history to score an NFL touchdown and hit a major league home run in the same week. The press made a big thing out of that, but I wasn't surprised. From the very beginning I was on the fast track, and that's where I wanted to be. Still, it would be a long time before I would feel like I could slow down and relax a little bit.

I left the Yankees in 1990 and signed with the Atlanta Braves so I could work a little closer to home. I played for the Braves during baseball season and the Atlanta Falcons in football season, and that continued through the 1993 season. By that time I realized I wasn't going anywhere with the Falcons. The challenges and the opportunities just weren't coming.

Even though they had some good coaches and a lot of great players on the field, for some reason the Falcons couldn't put together a play-off season, and I had a lot to prove. I wasn't going to be content just hanging around a mid-level team for the rest of my career, so I decided to make what sportswriters would later call my "celebrated national tour," flying from Miami to New Orleans to L.A., and from Kansas City to Dallas, and eventually to San Francisco looking for a new home.

I have more to say about that later on, but for now just let me say that I decided to go to San Francisco. After meeting with the owner, Eddie DeBartolo, I knew it was the right decision. That year, the 1994–95 season, turned out to be one of the most outstanding seasons of my professional life. I had over 300 yards in interceptions and was able to tie the 49ers' single-season team record of 3 interception returns for scores, with plays of 74, 93, and 90 yards. I was named NFC Defensive Player of the Week in my first start. I had 8 tackles that game and iced the 49ers' victory with a 74-yard interception return and a touchdown with 32 seconds left on the clock. But the whole season went like that, right up through the Super Bowl. It was an outstanding year.

After that incredible season in San Francisco, some people were saying that I was personally responsible for the 49ers' NFC Championship victory as well as the big Super Bowl win. But even that kind of praise didn't give me any peace. I still couldn't relax. The more they hyped it, the more it just intensified my appetite. I was hungry for more and more and more, and after winning a Super Bowl I realized that I had a new challenge and something even bigger to prove.

I was thinking, *Okay, if I'm all that, why not just go to Dallas or some other team and see if it's true. Can I be "the factor" on some other team? Can I be the one who makes "the difference" in another division championship and another Super Bowl season?*

I talked to my attorney, Eugene Parker, and he talked with Jerry Jones, the Cowboys owner who had already said he'd like to get me to come down to Dallas. A few days later we flew down there to look things over. Even though I already knew I wanted to make a change, we took the tour, met the players and coaches, and just generally looked things over, and it was all very impressive.

For one thing, guys like Michael Irvin, who I already loved and respected, were very encouraging to me. I played opposite Michael all the way through college when he was at Miami and I was at Florida State. Most of the time Michael was the best receiver on the field, and when I called him to ask about playing for Dallas he said the Cowboys really treated their players right and they wanted me to come.

Mike assured me that the coaches, players, management, and everybody else wanted me in Dallas, so by the time Eugene and I got into it, I was already feeling pretty confident about going there. They said the things I wanted to hear, and when Jerry Jones made his substantial (and highly publicized) contract offer of $35 million, it was a perfect fit! Reporters called it the biggest move in the three-year history of free agency, and that was fine by me.

Even though Michael Irvin, Troy Aikman, and Emmitt Smith had all been rivals of mine in college, I knew they were good people, and they were proven winners. They weren't going to mess with me about something like that, so if they told me that nobody on the team was going to be envious or nasty about me coming over to Dallas, I believed them.

But furthermore, Mike told me that the fans would be excited to see me come to Dallas. Everybody knows there's no love lost between Dallas and San Francisco, and that was something to think about. At least, it was a factor in the back of my mind. I didn't want to have to fight the fans, but Michael assured me that wouldn't be a problem. And it wasn't.

When I finally met with Jerry Jones following a Reds-Cubs game, I knew I was going to go ahead and do it. I was so impressed when I talked to Mr. Jones because he was honest and right up-front about everything. A few days before that I saw him on some live national press conference, and I heard him saying, "Deion Sanders is going to play for the Dallas Cowboys, and we're going to get him." And I remember thinking, *Okay, Boss!* and suddenly it was like, "Show me the money!"

It's funny because that was a strike year in major league baseball, and I decided to spend part of that time doing something fun, and I wanted to fulfill another one of my dreams, by cutting a rap album. I wrote and performed my own songs and put it all together with a band in the studio, and when it was all done, my agent signed me onto a mini-rap tour with the new CD, *Deion Sanders: Prime Time.* So for the next several weeks I was able to tour the country.

I always had this sort of rapper image and I thought it would be fun to do something other than football and baseball in my life. So I was thinking I could do music and rap. It was one more challenge that I could take on and conquer. I had the chance to prove I could do it, and it was like a dream come true. And to make it even more fun, one of the singles on the album, "Must Be the Money," hit the top-10 charts and was getting airtime all over the country.

Must Be the Money!

You know, ever since I turned pro in 1989,
when I signed the dotted line, ·
it was strange when things changed,
for the better and for the worse.
So I called my mama, and she said,
"Baby, must be the money! . . .

Must be the money!" Yeah, yeah.
It's got to be, 'cause I got people coming . . .

Must be the money that's turning them on;
Must be the money. You know what can go wrong?
Must be the money. That keeps me lookin' cold.
Must be the money. That's got me rollin' on the stroll.
Limousines and first class I fly.
I'm living large and you know I can't deny . . .
Must be the money!

I wrote the song myself, pretty much saying to people: *You know, it must be the money that's turning so many people on to Deion Sanders. It has to be the money*, I said, *because I can't go wrong! It must be the money . . . that has to be the explanation for everything . . . because I know it can't be me!* That's pretty much what I was saying, but, as usual, the song got misinterpreted and some people thought I was just bragging about my fame and success. But the song went over well in the 'hood, anyway, like I knew it would.

So you gotta realize that during this time I was going all around the country on a tour bus with six beautiful women, our dancers, and it was really wild! We had a couple of strippers along—that's how they made their living, taking off their clothes—but being in that environment, away from my wife and kids, was not good for me, and I paid a price for it later. But we did it anyway. And it was right after that, when I got back from the music tour, that I started my tour to all the various NFL teams around the country to see where I wanted to play.

At the same time, lots of other teams were calling to see if they could make a deal. I don't even remember all the teams that called or what order they were in, but I really wanted to play for the Miami Dolphins with all my heart. It was close to home. My mother was a big football fan, and if I played for Miami that would have made it so much easier for her to make the trips to the games. She comes to all my games now, but it's a long way for her and she has to fly all over the country to see me play. So I decided I wanted to play for those guys so bad.

I would get excited just thinking about being back in Florida. I mean, I could fish every day, build myself a beautiful home down there. So I would get on the phone with Dan Marino, saying, "Man, tell those guys I really want to play down there!" But when it came time to make a deal, management tried to lowball me with their offer. So I put them on hold and started off on my celebrated national tour. My good friend, the super rap star M. C. Hammer, and his brother, Louis Burrell, came with me and we went to New Orleans and all over the place.

One reason I took Hammer with me was that I really liked to be with him. But part of it was calculated, of course. We wanted things to look a little bigger and flashier than they might have seemed otherwise. It's not just Prime Time coming to town, you know, but Hammer and a whole bunch of celebrities, just to blow things up!

When I walked out on the field at the Super Dome in New Orleans, the fans just went crazy. It was great! The players and coaches down there all knew I liked to fish so they set up a special day and took me out fishing in their boat, but I got sick as a dog. What they didn't realize was that I like to go bass fishing, which is mostly on much smaller lakes, but they took me way out on Lake Ponchartrain and I just completely lost it!

Those folks were really good to me, and ultimately they offered me the most money up to that time. But I wasn't ready to stop looking at that point, so from there we went on to Kansas City and they were good people, too, but I knew there wasn't much chance I was going to sign with them. Derek Thomas and Neil Smith were good friends of mine and they were glad to see me, but it was pretty obvious that the other guys on the team didn't want me there. They barely even spoke to me, and I knew immediately that it wasn't going to be a good fit.

With the salary cap being what it is, some of those guys probably thought they'd have to take a pay cut if I came to town, so they weren't all that glad to see me! But whatever the reason, the visit there was short and sweet and I headed for California.

The Season That Was

San Francisco was the last stop on my tour, and as soon as I met with Eddie DeBartolo I knew it was a match. He said they didn't have much money to give me, but I realized that if I could make the sacrifice and go out there, I could fulfill another one of my dreams. I think the main thing I wanted to accomplish with that tour was to sign on with a team that really had a chance to make it to the Super Bowl, and I knew the 49ers had about as good a chance as anybody.

The Cowboys had called my agent a few weeks before that, but Jerry Jones wasn't serious enough about getting me to play for them at that time. That narrowed it down, and the visit with Mr. DeBartolo cinched it for me. We had a wonderful visit and I pretty much made my decision while I was there.

Ironically, the minute the plane touched down in Atlanta, my portable phone started ringing and it was the Miami Dolphins, saying, "Man, we really want you to come to Miami. Whatever you want, we'll give it to you." Later Dan Marino called me and said, "Yeah, Prime, they want you, man. Come on down here. They'll pay whatever you want."

It turned out they had just played their last preseason game before the regular season and Drew Bledsoe and the Cincinnati Bengals had blasted them for something like 300 yards passing, and they were still in shock. Suddenly they realized they needed a good cornerback who could make sure that kind of thing would never happen again. Fans and sponsors were calling them saying, "Forget the price tag! Go get Deion Sanders, right now!" But as much as I wanted to go there, I had already made up my mind to go to San Francisco and I couldn't go back on a deal.

The whole time I was on the road, my main endorsement, Nike Athletic Shoes, kept asking me, "Deion, where do you think you're going to play next year?" and I said, "Man, I'm going to Miami!" So before I could let them know of my change of plans they had already made up shoes with Miami colors for me. That's how bad I wanted to go to Miami. But once I made my decision to go with the 49ers, and once I had given Mr. DeBartolo my word that I was coming, there was no way I was going back on it. So that's how I landed in San Francisco.

The other part of it, however, is that there was so much tension during all of this. You can't even imagine what I was going through. I almost went crazy, going back and forth, back and forth. I wanted to make the right decision, not just for my sake, because it also meant that I'd be moving my whole family out to the Bay Area. Also, if I had signed with any of the other teams I visited on that trip, I would probably have signed a long-term deal. More than likely it would have been the last move of my career, so I wanted it to be right for everybody's sake. But the 49ers let me have a one-year contract, and that meant I'd be free to move in one year if I didn't like it there for any reason.

Some people have this image of NFL players sitting at home, relaxing around the pool while their attorneys are out there making deals and getting their heads bashed in, but that's really not how it is with me. Whenever I'm putting something together, my attorney and I are a team. For one thing, Eugene and I have always been on the same page. He knows my thought processes, my likes and dislikes, and he pretty well knows what I'm going to say about the various deals we're offered even before he asks. So we really do work well as a team. But it also means I feel the pressure a lot more than some other players, and there were times during the big tour that I thought I was going to collapse.

I wanted to make sure that Carolyn and the kids never had to go through all the pressures of my job or the various business deals I was involved in, so I never took those things home with me. At least, I tried not to. I never showed them my disappointments or hurts. Still, I was confused a lot of times about what I wanted to do and where I wanted to go, and since I wasn't sharing my thoughts with anybody, I would have migraines and things like that. But I never took my work home with me, and I never let it boil over.

I was just bottling it up inside, as I have done all my life. I didn't want to let that stuff come out. That's probably one of the reasons that Carolyn and I later got a divorce, because she never really knew me. She knew Prime Time and I think that's who she really loved—the lights, the glitter, the spectacle, the money.

Ironically, when Jerry Jones made his offer, he wasn't the highest bidder. I have to be honest about that. Al Davis, the general manager of the Raiders, made the best offer but no one ever knew that. But I had to think about a lot of things at that time. I loved the Raiders. I loved Al Davis. I grew up watching Lester Hayes and I really liked the Raiders style when I was a kid, so I was inclined to go there.

But I never liked California and the taxes and the cost of living out there would have made any deal I signed much less valuable than a comparable deal anywhere else. So I chose to come to Dallas. And the main thing in the back of my mind was this feeling that I still wanted to prove I could take two different teams to the Super Bowl in two successive years. I'd taken the first step with the 49ers, and now it was time to see if I could do it again with the Dallas Cowboys.

The thing about it is that I had a lot of time to relax because I had to have ankle surgery at the end of baseball season. I was out for three or four weeks and couldn't play at all. I couldn't even practice, so I had to rehab my ankle and try to get ready for football.

Was that a little scary? No, not really. I knew it was messed up during baseball season, so they just did the surgery and that was cool. I remember the night we played the Chicago Cubs. That's the night we did the deal with Dallas. Mr. Jones and his key guys all flew in and we signed the papers that night.

When word got around in California that I was talking about possibly going to Dallas next season, it was like the San Francisco earthquake all over again! Suddenly the fans hated me! I was still playing baseball for the San Francisco Giants, but now I was going to play football for the Cowboys, and you gotta realize that's just craziness. They hated me! It got to the point that some of my homeys were sitting in the outfield every night because guys in the stands were saying such crazy stuff and throwing batteries on the field. When it was too rough, my friends would get into fights and all kinds of stuff.

One night they got into it and knocked some guy out. Beat him half to death, and the guy turned out to be a policeman who had been drinking and he didn't have his badge, and they had to go to court because of that. It was nonsense, but the fans were just all over me, and I couldn't wait to get out of there! I was having two- and three-day migraines.

The team doctor would have to come over to the hotel room and inject me with a pain medicine to put me to sleep, and I remember I would fall asleep within a minute of the injection. When I'd wake up the next day, I would be dazed, dizzy, out of it. But the headaches were so tremendous because of the stress.

At that time, Carolyn and I were pretty much separated. Her mother passed away and I was leaving soon, but I couldn't leave. If I had even gone out of town long enough to go to the funeral, I felt they would have just murdered me out there in San Francisco. I realize now that I should have gone to the funeral, but I was just concentrating on finishing out my contract and I only had three more weeks to play before I could get out of there. I was hoping I could just hold on for three more weeks until I was officially released by the owners and got my last big check.

Maybe if I had gone with Carolyn to the funeral things might have worked out differently, but the pressures were just outrageous at that time and I really doubt if I could have done anything to turn it around.

chapter nine

A NEW DIRECTION

It was one for the record books. Everything I touched turned to gold, but inside, I was broken and totally defeated. I remember being on the practice field with the 49ers and thinking to myself, *This is going to be the best season of my career.* I was on my way to being named Defensive Player of the Year, but inside I was totally empty. Just losing it in the middle of the season. I remember sitting at the back of the practice field one afternoon, away from everybody, and tears were running down my face.

I was saying to myself, *This is so meaningless. I'm so unhappy. We're winning every week and I'm playing great, but I'm not happy.* It wasn't because of Carolyn or the kids, I just wasn't happy. And then we played a Monday Night game against the Vikings near the end of the season, and I remember telling one of the 49ers coaches, "I'm leaving, man. I'll see y'all in a few days."

I spent the night in Minnesota that night then caught the first plane out the next morning and headed back to my place in Atlanta. I needed to clear my head, so I went fishing for a few days because fishing was always the closest thing to the peace of God I ever had. That's why I always enjoyed it so much. So I just laid back for a while and tried to rest, but when I came back it was still there. The hurt just wouldn't go away.

I remember winning the Super Bowl that year, and that night after the game I was the first one out of the locker room, the first one to the press conference, and the first one to go home. And I remember my wife, Carolyn, saying to me, "Baby, you just won the Super Bowl! Don't you have a party downstairs or something to go to?" And I just said, "Nah," and I rolled over and went to sleep. That was the same week I bought myself a brand new $275 thousand Lamborghini and I hadn't even driven a mile before I realized, *No, that's not it. That's not what I'm looking for. It's got to be something else. I'm so hungry!*

That's when the Lord was really calling me. There was nobody going through it with me. It was just me, one-on-one with God. I tried running from it and running from it, and even when I was playing baseball the following year in Cincinnati, the Lord kept calling me, pulling me, drawing me along. And that was the season they went out on strike.

I tried everything. Parties, women, buying expensive jewelry and gadgets, and nothing helped. There was no peace. I mean I was playing great. Every time I would turn on the TV I could see myself on three or four commercials. At one time I think I was on five different commercials at the same time. You see yourself, the kids see you, you've got all this media attention and everything the world has to offer, but no peace, no joy, just emptiness inside.

The Bible describes it in the first chapter of Ecclesiastes as chasing after the wind, and that's exactly what it was like. I tried to buy myself something to make me happy and I was even emptier than before, because I could see that nothing could possibly satisfy the hunger that was deep down inside of me.

I would try to remember the dreams of that seven-year-old boy from Fort Myers, Florida, and tell myself that I had made it. I was there. I was at the top of my game and I had everything that anybody could ever want, but nothing changed. That's when you turn to the women, and you say, *Okay, let me get this woman and have sex with her, and then I'll be happy.* But that doesn't do it, so the next thing you know you've got two women; but nothing, nothing, nothing.

So then I decided I wanted to be a rap star. I put together that deal, cut my album, and went on tour. But I felt nothing, no peace, and all this time I was searching in all the wrong place for an answer. All I could do was stay busy, occupy my time, doing whatever I could to keep working so the feelings of emptiness wouldn't come to haunt me.

I'd see a beautiful woman who was a challenge and I'd end up conquering her and I'd say to myself, *Aw, man, this is not it!* I'd go to Hollywood and hang out with celebrities and actresses I knew out there, and I'd conquer them, and, *No, this ain't it either!* Next thing I knew I'd be lying up in bed with two, three, four women, and realizing, *I'm just getting farther and farther away. And this is definitely not it!*

So I would buy myself another car, more suits, more expensive clothes, more jewelry, more of everything, and I already knew before I got out of the mall that it wasn't going to make me happy. I tried throwing myself into my career, into sports, trying to see how far I could go, and when I achieved every goal I could think of, I was right back where I started. Empty, empty, empty, and nothing I did could touch that deep loneliness inside of me. I was just running. I couldn't stop.

The pain was horrible. Inconceivable. Anyone who has never had that experience can't begin to imagine what it was like to be in my shoes at that time. It was just crushing pain. I didn't know it then, but I know now that I have a high calling on my life. Not just a regular calling to be a Christian, to go to church and serve the Lord, but a calling that's deeper and bigger and more compelling than anything I could have imagined just a few years ago.

One More Chance

After my agent made our deal and the discussions were concluded, I signed with Dallas and went on down to check it out. We put on some kind of show! Press conferences are a little bit like sideshows, but that's usually what you have to do because you never get a second chance to make a first impression. When I was getting ready that morning I was going through my wardrobe, saying, "Okay, Dallas, let me get the pinstripe suit here. Let me wear this and that, and it's like 'Showtime!' All right, the entertainment is here, and Prime Time is getting ready to come on out!" The press conferences went over really well. And once I did that I wouldn't have to go back and play baseball for a while.

Carolyn had come with me, and over the next several weeks we made the move to Dallas step by step. We thought that maybe now it would be possible for us to start fresh again and get things back together. We were moving to a new city, getting a new start, and I thought for a while that maybe Carolyn was thinking we could get it all back together.

The transition went fine, but I tend to be very impatient and I want to get on with it. Carolyn came to Dallas ahead of me and she had Realtors showing her around, and what she wanted to do was to have the house pretty well settled before I got there. She wanted to narrow down the choices to the best two or three so we could make a decision as soon as I got into town. She was down there looking for houses while I was still playing baseball.

The Realtors let us know the best places to live. They let us know where other players lived in our area and stuff like that. But it was during this time, when Carolyn was making all these real estate decisions, that her mother passed away, and that turned out to be a major challenge for both of us. Originally there was one particular house that she really liked, but we thought it was too big and too expensive, so she thought we would end up taking one of the other choices. But she was going through so much pain at that time because of her mother's death, I decided to try to get her the house she liked so much.

So I got on the phone with the banker and I said, "Now, come on, man, you've got to do better than that," and I haggled a little and bargained with him over the price and all that, and before long we were able to make a better deal. That's the house I have now, and when I bought it, it was like my gift to her for all she had been through with her mother's passing. So we finally moved in while I was still in rehab with the Cowboys, and we were trying to put the pieces together.

I was really relaxed because I was just getting to know the people and the system in Dallas. By the time I was rehabbed and ready to play, we were already into the regular season and everybody was speculating about when I'd be ready to play and which team I'd be starting against.

Ironically, it turned out to be the Atlanta Falcons, my old team. That was my first game for the Cowboys. There was a lot of speculation about what would happen in the media, but by the time the game actually arrived it didn't mean as much as it had the year before when I was at San Francisco. That game had made a lot more news because some of the Falcons said some really nasty things about me the week before the 49ers game. Going back to play against the team I had just left was big news in the '94 season. Of course, I felt we were going to win because I was with a superior team and Atlanta wasn't doing much that year. But even though I wasn't all that concerned about the game, some of my old teammates were still carrying a grudge.

One of my best friends on the Falcons was André Rison, but he said some things about me—out of hurt more than anything else I think—and he shouldn't have done that. I don't fault him for it until this day because I left him and I know what he was feeling at the time. We made up later and today I consider him one of my closest friends, but it was stressful for a while and one thing just led to another. He's a tremendous guy and a great football player. But we got into a fight on the field during that game and it was wrong. It should never have happened.

But people know my style of play; I'm very aggressive and I rushed at André during one particular play and I caught him up under the chin. I told him I didn't mean to do that, it just happened. "Man, you know I don't play like that," I said. "You know I'm not a dirty player." But he didn't care. He was hurt, he was angry, and I guess he didn't believe me, because on the very next play he came after me.

I saw him coming and I guess I was still tense about the things he had said about me in the papers when he took what I felt was a cheap shot at me, so this time we really got into it on the field and we started fighting. To make matters worse, later in the same series the Falcons were getting close to the goal line when I snagged one and took an interception nearly 90 yards the other way, and of course I high-stepped and danced all the way into the end zone.

We ended up beating them really badly, and I ended up pulling a groin because I wasn't ready to run at that level yet. But the statements I made after the game made headlines all around the country. I was saying things like, "This is my house! I built this house, and it'll always be my house!" So that got a lot of play and it didn't endear me at all with the Atlanta fans!

But by the time we played them in Dallas, all that sort of personal rivalry had pretty much faded quiet. The Falcons were down, Dallas was up, and I knew we were going to beat them, so there wasn't any kind of repeat of what had happened the year before.

I had already been to two different teams in my football career, and I had been a Pro-Bowler for both of them. I knew the fans were watching me. Let's face it, I had gotten an exorbitant amount of money so they probably thought that I felt I had to prove myself. But why would I have to prove myself when all I was going to do was sit out there on the corner and just dare anybody to throw the ball to my side!?

Fans who know football know that's what they pay me for, because I'm denying the opponent the ability to throw the football to one whole side of the field. So it was never like I had to prove myself to anybody, let alone to myself. I think I probably felt some of that in San Francisco, but not in Dallas.

My main concern was to put the past behind me and be the man I was supposed to be—Deion Sanders, not Prime Time. Prime Time was the persona I had created in college to help me make it big in the pros. It had worked, big time, and worked so well I couldn't shake it when I wanted to move on and secure my mother's future.

Once I got to the NFL, I really wanted to let all that stuff go. In my own mind, Prime Time was basically over and done with, but the fans wouldn't let him just fade away gracefully. When I do commercials, I still have to do that sort of thing. I use the swagger and let all that boastful personality come out because it sells. But that's not the way I play anymore, and it's not the way I think of myself. What you see out there now is Deion Sanders: That's the real me, not some manufactured character.

The Last Straw

Even though we had been together for several years, Carolyn and I weren't actually married until 1996. But it was like as soon as we got married things started going wrong. Within months of our wedding she filed for divorce on two separate occasions, the first time because of a scandal that broke around the country and caused us both a lot of grief. I had gone out to make a Pepsi commercial in Los Angeles, and while I was there I messed around with a girl who later claimed that she was pregnant with my child.

Now, this young lady already had two kids by two different athletes, and she was getting child support from both of them. But a few months after I had gone back home and things were moving along pretty smooth, I got word that she had been calling my friends saying she was pregnant with my baby. But I'm saying, "No way, Baby! Not me!" But she was saying she wanted me to give her $500,000 or she was going public with the whole thing, and I said, "You've gotta be out of your mind, girl! You know that's not my kid. If you try this, I'll just take my chances! You can go ahead and go public for all I care."

Next thing I know, my attorney gets a call from her attorney and they say they're going to hit me with a nasty scandal unless I cooperate and pay the half-million. Obviously she didn't know how I was about money. So, again I said, "Go ahead! I don't care." But then I remember getting the call on my cell phone one night at football camp, and it was Carolyn. She was in tears, saying she had just seen this special on *Hard Copy*, and it was some young woman saying I had fathered her baby in California.

I was sure it wasn't my kid, so I had blood tests taken to confirm that I couldn't be the father. Sure enough, I wasn't, but the damage had been done. I drove home that night and tried to comfort my wife, but she was about to go crazy, and it was a wild time. The upshot was that this experience brought Carolyn to the point where she demanded that we get some kind of counseling. She originally wanted to go see this well-known pastor she knew about in Dallas, but when she called his office to set up an appointment he was out of town at a national Promise Keepers event. So then she called Bishop Jakes's office, and that was when I started getting in touch with God. That was in 1996.

We went for two or three sessions with the bishop before I said I wasn't going back anymore. I didn't enjoy it at all. I was more upset after we left than when we got there. And it wasn't just because I was having to talk about things I didn't want to deal with, but I was sitting there, trying to tell the truth, trying to be honest, and I felt that Carolyn wasn't telling the whole truth.

I felt she was putting everything on me and I was the victim. I didn't want any part of it, so I refused to go back. But, out of curiosity more than anything, I started reading a couple of Bishop Jakes's books, *Can You Stand to Be Blessed?* and *Loose That Man and Let Him Go!* And before I knew what was happening, I was really getting into it. I started buying books for the guys on the football team, saying, "Man, you gotta read this! This guy is good! He's really getting into my life."

I was reading all the time, and I couldn't put it down. It was like the Lord was getting me ready for the change that was about to come. It wasn't anything I was seeing on television, and it wasn't Bishop Jakes's preaching in church that was doing it, because I wasn't receiving any of that. I was going to church, but I had too many defenses set up to be able to take in what I was hearing.

In fact, the day I left for spring training in Tampa, I drove down to the Bishop's church, the Potter's House, that morning. I just wanted to hear Bishop preach one sermon before I left. I remember driving back straight from the nightclub I owned at that time at about six o'clock in the morning. I went home, got showered, changed clothes, and then drove to church by myself. I didn't even go to the front of the house or say anything to Carolyn about it. I just went.

Something about me couldn't accept what Bishop Jakes was saying face-to-face, but whenever I could read it for myself, in his books, then I was open to receive the message. But I never contacted Bishop to talk about any of it. I was trying to find the answers for myself. And that's when all these other things started happening.

My life was falling apart. I was pretty much at the bottom during all this. My baseball game started to fall off and before long some of the guys on the team could see that something was wrong. But I don't think anybody ever guessed that my life was in shambles. I was out of town, of course, so I couldn't get back to see Bishop Jakes.

It was during all of this that Carolyn's lawyers were filing papers on me in the middle of the baseball field and stupid stuff like that. I called her and asked, "Why do you let these idiots do stuff like that?" But she said she didn't care. She just wanted this exorbitant amount of money in the divorce settlement. I went off like a rocket. "Man, I didn't know you were on the meter while you were living with me?!" I said. It was just crazy.

Cry of the Heart

I was struggling with just about everything in my life. My attorney could see what I was going through and he tried to help as much as he could, but I was so disappointed and disturbed about the way things were falling apart that I wouldn't listen to his advice most of the time. He talked about his faith, how Jesus gave his life purpose, and things like that, but I wasn't ready to receive any of that.

Eugene had been with Campus Crusade for Christ while he was in college in California, and after that he became a full-time staffer with a ministry called Athletes in Action. Somewhere along the way, he decided to go on to law school and when he finished with his law degree, he moved up to Fort Wayne, Indiana, and he was doing ministry work even while he was building his practice.

So when I was really in the valley, I saw something in Eugene. It wasn't so much what he was saying as how he was living. He was different, and he had a peace I had never experienced. Sometimes a bunch of us would get together and play a little basketball, and whenever we wanted to know who had fouled or who knocked the ball out, I could always turn to Eugene and get an honest answer. He never cheated, never lied, and I began to see that whatever he had was something I really admired.

But at some point I came to the conclusion that there was no way out for me. I keep a notebook with me when I'm traveling and I've always written poetry and lyrics and tried to write down what I was going through. Earlier in my life they were mostly happy and optimistic. I still had hope. But by this time they had become very dark and morose. I realize now that even my lyrics that sounded happy and colorful at that time—about clouds and sunny days—often expressed the darkness and emptiness in my soul.

In one of them, called "Who Are You?" I was wrestling with the idea of love and relationships. I wrote:

WHO ARE YOU?

Who are you?
Didn't we used to love each other?
Now we're miles apart under the covers.
Who are you? I don't know you anymore.

Didn't we used to have an ungodly rapport?
I never wanted you out of my sight—
Now I can't stand you near.
Who have you become, my dear?

I wanted to grow old and gray together, forever,
But I soon found out you were much more clever.
Who are you to take advantage of my heart?
I should have known from the very start.

I don't know you at all anymore.
The things you've done have left my heart torn.
Didn't we used to do things with each other?
I don't recall the last time you've truly been a lover.

Who are you? Aren't you the mother of my kids?
Or are you someone not happy with what you did?
I could go on and on with many more questions;
But really all I want to know is, who have you become?

In another one of those verses that I wrote on the way to an out-of-town
game with the Cowboys, I was in a similar mood, but I was beginning to
think about life and death and the chances of ever getting any answers to
life's big questions. In the one below called, "Where Am I?" I think you
may get some idea of what I was feeling at the time. I said:

WHERE AM I?

It's so beautiful to see what a bird sees—
To another level. High above the clouds
What to see? Peace is the only reflection
Your face resembles here.

High above the clouds there is no crime,
No murders, no rape, no living in vain.
It's so warm but cool, moving slowly but fast.
Life is truly special high above the clouds.

The feeling of security is false, because
you may fall through. No, it will catch you.
That's how you feel, high above the clouds.
Why can't I move to this place—

Where no man or woman has ever gone—
or have they? I hear singing. I feel joy.
I feel triumph high above the clouds.
I can lie down or fall asleep so deep that

I may never wake, high above the clouds.
It's not far for my soul to take. I've decided
Where I must rest. High above the clouds
Would truly be best. Where am I?

I think that writing verses like that was good for me. But it was also one of the first times I began to consider the possibility that there might be some kind of peaceful and final solution to all my unhappiness and disappointment.

My Uncle Billy was traveling with me during baseball season, looking after me and making sure I was all right. He had been through a lot with me and he usually knew how to handle me, but he was starting to get worried. Billy talked to Eugene Parker on the phone several times and just about the time when I was feeling I couldn't keep up the pretense any longer, Eugene flew up to spend a few days, and that's when I took the plunge—literally—over that cliff in Cincinnati in my beautiful black Mercedes.

chapter ten

A HIGH CALLING

fter I drove my car over the cliff, Billy got a call from the police and both he and Eugene came down to the wreck, and after they settled everything with the police, I went back with them to the house. But Eugene was obviously angry with me and as soon as we walked in the door he started talking to me, as seriously as anybody ever has in my entire life.

He warned me about the consequences of what I had just done and told me that if I didn't get a grip on my actions he was going to have me locked up for my own good. I thought he was just kidding, but he assured me that he was serious. As my attorney, he had the authority to put me under a doctor's care for a long time if he thought I might be at risk of hurting myself.

I think the main reason that made such a strong impression on me is because I trusted Eugene so much and I knew he would never lie to me or exaggerate in any way. But I was still feeling terrible on the inside, so Billy called my mother in Fort Myers and she, in turn, called my aunt. So Scoodie jumped on the first plane out of Atlanta and was in Cincinnati within four hours of the accident. She and Billy traveled with me for the next few weeks. Scoodie got a room in the same hotel, just like one of the players, and she says that for a while she became the unknown Cincinnati Red.

Through all of that, Eugene could see could see I was dealing with a lot of grief, and one night he said that his pastor back in Indiana had a good friend who lived up in Columbus, Ohio, a guy named Pastor David Forbes, and he was a big Dallas Cowboys fans and he really wanted to meet me. It turns out that at the same time he was saying that to me, Eugene was telling Pastor Forbes that I was in the area and I really wanted to meet him and all that! So Eugene was playing it both ways!

Well, I had agreed to attend a celebrity basketball game up there, so I got on the phone with Pastor Forbes and I said, "Yeah, man, just meet me at the basketball game at halftime and we'll get to talk a little bit." So he came at halftime, got my attention, and we went back to the locker room and talked, and talked, and talked, and we didn't come out until the game was over and the lights were off. Everybody else had gone home and our cars were the last ones in the lot.

We talked that long and I had never opened up like that with any pastor in my life before that night. We got deep into some of the things I was dealing with and we developed a close friendship that day. He said he was coming back the next week, and at the same time Bishop Jakes was calling me in Cincinnati, so God was starting to send people into my life.

I started asking Eugene what it meant to be a believer in Jesus Christ and he was telling me about being saved, and about this time I got a call from a guy I used to play with on the 49ers, Mark Logan. He was playing for the Washington Redskins and he said he was planning on being in Cincinnati that night and would like to meet with me. So after the game Mark came to the ballpark and we met.

We drove down to an IHOP and we must have sat there for three or four hours. I really respected Mark as a person and as a Christian. You know, we always have chapel before the football game, and I remember one time Mark prayed in chapel and I said, like, "Oh, my goodness!" When he was praying I was like, "Umm, umm, yeah!" He was really laying it down!

But Mark is a good-lookin' guy, a dresser. I used to call him Denzel. So later, after the prayer, I said, "Denzel, man, you really tore it up in there!" His prayer really touched me, and I thought it was interesting that, all this time later, he would suddenly show up in Cincinnati and come over to share with me about the Lord.

After we ate dinner, we sat there in the same seats for hours, and he was telling me about how the Lord was working in his life. At one point he asked me, "Deion, are you saved?" And I said, "No, man, I can't say that I am. But my attorney has been asking me the same question." Of course, Eugene knew that I wasn't saved, but I had been reading up on it, and after talking with Mark I went home and went to bed, and this stuff was really on my mind.

I was lying there in bed about four o'clock in the morning when I was awakened by these awesome lights in my room. In my testimony I say it was like a 747 had landed beside my bed, and there was this incredible rush of wind that felt like a helicopter had come in with it.

I remember opening my eyes just the slightest bit and saying, "God, if that's You, take me! Take me, Lord," and I was trembling all over. Before long it was silent and the lights disappeared, and later that night I got up and opened my Bible to a passage that said, "If you confess with your mouth the Lord Jesus and believe in your heart that God has raised Him from the dead, you will be saved. For with the heart one believes unto righteousness, and with the mouth confession is made unto salvation." That's Romans 10, verses 9 and 10, and the words hit me like a ton of bricks. I knew they were meant for me, and at that precise moment I was delivered.

I put my trust in Jesus and asked Him into my life. And as soon as I realized what I had done I was so excited I had to tell somebody, so I got on the phone and called my attorney and said, "Eugene, I did it!"

Now Eugene must have been scared out of his mind, with me calling at that time of the night, especially after all I'd been through during the past year. So he said, "What, Deion? What did you do?"

I said, "I got saved!"

That was the beginning, and Eugene was excited to know I'd found the Lord at last. But I'll never, never forget that experience. It was bright as Christmas, and it was like a real visitation from God.

After that, little things started to change. I was still going through all the mess, but the more I read and the more I learned about the Christian life, the easier it was to deal with the bad stuff. I was reading all these books written by Bishop Jakes. One of the people at the Potter's House in Dallas was sending me books and tapes and all kinds of stuff, and I was getting up and going to bed listening to tapes of the Bishop's sermons.

In the car, at practice, eating dinner: Wherever I was I was listening to Bishop. Before the game, on the field doing sit-ups, I'd have my headphones on listening to Bishop. Pastor Forbes was close, too, and he would come up and visit me from time to time and talk to me about growing stronger in the Lord. I remember one particular trip when he came down and tried to minister to Carolyn and me, but I don't think she was ready for reconciliation at that time.

I wanted to talk about getting back together with Carolyn, but from her tone I could tell that she was full-fledged into this divorce thing. But I was just feeding myself, day by day, constantly growing in the faith. Then there would be a storm there and I would stumble, and another one and another one, and each time I would stumble. But I knew I had to keep on going.

The day after my birthday, on the tenth of August 1997, that was the first time I ever gave my testimony, when I spoke to the people at the Church of God in Christ in Cincinnati. After getting up and testifying about what God had done for me, I felt better than I'd ever felt in my life. Telling about the trials and tribulations of the professional athlete, and all the Delilahs and Jezebels I'd run into, it was like the Lord spoke to me and said, "Don't be ashamed of Me." He told me to have the courage to go on and speak about what He had done in my life, and it was just a complete and total transformation that began to work inside of me.

Good for Evil

During that whole time it was really rough for me. It was as if Satan was trying to punch a hole in my defenses and the Lord was giving him a free hand. I remember playing in the outfield during a Reds game down in Houston, and there was some loudmouth out there yelling at me, "Deion, you *#*!*?* jerk. You garbage. You suck!" I didn't know if I was going to be able to take much more of that, so at one point at the end of the inning I ran over to the wall where this guy was sitting, and when I was about ten feet away I just said, "Hey, man, you know what? God loves you. God bless you!" After that I didn't hear a peep out of him the rest of the night.

But we had another game down there the next night, and this time there was a whole group of them screaming obscenities and acting hateful, and I went over to where they were sitting and I said, "Man, I'm just

My first national championship wasn't at Florida State; it was with the Pop Warner League "Dynomites!" coached by Dave Capel (back row, far left). I was the star running back, and wore number 29 at that time (top middle).

This school photo was taken in 1975—before "Prime Time".

Here's me in my Pee Wee baseball uniform, 1979.

At the dedication ceremony when the City of Fort Myers declared
"Deion Sanders Day," I was accompanied by my stepfather, Will Knight

. . . and my father, Buck Sanders.

After another big game with my mother, Connie, and my father, Mims "Buck" Sanders. This was my freshman year at FSU.

In 1988, my final season at Florida State, I presented
Coach Capel with mementos from all my college
playoff bowl appearances.

I never doubted that one day I would keep my promise and build my mother her dream
home. But the day she moved into the new house at Gateway was a big one for all of us.

In my first game for the Dallas Cowboys.

My son, Deion Luwynn, Jr., is four years younger than Deiondra, but he's got personality beyond his years. I nicknamed him Bucky in honor of my father, Daddy Buck.

My daughter, Deiondra, is every ounce the young lady. When she came into our lives, in 1990, I began to see my role as a father and as a man with new eyes.

There's nothing I'd rather do than spend time with Deiondra, age 8, and Bucky, age 4. They love all kinds of sports, games, playing in the backyard, and just doing things together. Best of all, they love the Lord just as I do.

so thankful to be here. God is good, and He loves you too. God bless y'all!"

As I trotted back to my position in the outfield, one of those guys stood up and yelled at me, "Hey, Deion, you don't have to get personal!" That really got to them. I never heard another word from them after that either.

It wasn't too much later that my back went out and it was really hurting me. I was saying, "Oh, Lord, not this!" Here was a real test of my faith. I realized that I've still got circumstances: I'm reaping what I've sown before. I still had some things I'd have to get through. But I remember being so down because I couldn't even play baseball. I was sitting on the bench—and this was when I knew that God was really with me, and He was really doing something in me.

I was sitting on the bench one night, in my uniform, watching the game. I couldn't even stand up to watch it because my back was hurting so bad. But as I was sitting there, I looked up and saw this guy in the stands reaching for a home run ball and he fell behind the wall and landed on his head. My eyes shot open and immediately God lifted me up and I ran around through the tunnel as fast as I could. I kneeled by this guy and laid hands on him and started to pray.

Within seconds people were running out from all over the place and they said they had an ambulance on the way. A few minutes later I said I'd like to speak to the guy if he came around. Sure enough, he sort of woke up a little bit and looked around and someone said to him, "Deion Sanders would like to speak to you." So I kneeled down beside him and I just said, "God is good, man, and He loves you. You're still alive and you're still here. So have faith. He's going to take care of you."

So there I was, just ministering to this guy while he was lying there on the ground, and after a few minutes I headed on back to the locker room, and on the way there I was crying like a child. Like a baby! I went to my locker and got down on my knees, and I was just sobbing with the love that God had given me for this man. The love of Jesus was in me and I was feeling all this guy's pain and pressure, and I just submitted myself and said, "Lord, please touch this man's life and heal him and give him strength to come through this terrible fall."

I mean, it looked horrible. The guy had fallen headfirst from the second deck and by all rights he should have been dead. But by some miracle, he was still alive, and a little while later when I went back out to the bench they flashed a message on the scoreboard that the fan who had fallen was in the hospital and he was going to be all right. So I was really praising the Lord by that time.

But, you see, that was such a new experience for me. To have those kinds of feelings for another person and to know that God was just filling my heart with His love. But things like that were happening all the time. So when I was on the road, I always had my Bible along and I began to read and study the Word, and I couldn't get enough. I was hungry and thirsty for God's righteousness, and I was changing in every way you can imagine.

But that's just one example. From that time on, things like that started happening to me everywhere I went. Now when I'm on the road with the baseball team I'm usually out on my free time looking for churches to go visit. I'm taking Bishop Jakes's tapes with me, reading my Bible, constantly reading books about my spiritual walk, and I just can't get enough.

In the middle of all this I was still going through divorce proceedings, flying back and taking depositions. My back was still messed up, and all these things were taking a toll on my physical and mental strength. But God never deserted me. He always had His hand on me and carried me through.

It was unbelievable the things that were happening in my life. I had to come down to Dallas one time during baseball season to get my back checked out and Jerry Jones scheduled us for a press conference. The team doctors told everybody my back was going to be okay and I would be back to play football the next year. When I got up to speak I said that I gave God the credit for getting me up and on my feet again. But the press just attacked me after that, and they said things about me I couldn't believe I was hearing, putting me down, saying awful things and accusing me of hypocrisy and worse. Finally I said to one of the reporters, "Are you a Christian?" And he said, "No, I'm not." So I said, "Then you wouldn't understand, would you?"

That was a learning experience, but it really hurt me, nevertheless. I remember driving back home and thinking, *Man, with all the problems the Cowboys have had the last couple of years, with the accidents, the court cases, people going to jail, I would have thought the media would be glad to know that a player was really trying to walk the walk.* But the press weren't happy about my conversion. In fact, I think some of them were angry about it. And I thought, *That lets me know where they stand, and from now on I'll know what I'm dealing with.* At that moment I established a policy of only speaking to the press after football games. I don't talk to them on a daily basis anymore, and I never will.

The good news is that a lot of players on the team have come to Christ this past year, and they're trying to turn their lives around just like I am. So if the media wants to get an interview, they'd ought to get over it! I've taken a few cheap shots from other people since this all happened, including some of my friends, but that's to be expected.

I remember picking up the paper and seeing one story that said, "Will Deion be the same player now that he's found God?" and stupid stuff like that. I never listen to the talk shows anymore, but now and then one of my friends will call and tell me, "Man, they're talking about you like a dog, saying you're just faking." And I say, "If anybody says stuff like that, it only means they don't know Christ." Ultimately, none of it hurts me; but it did wake me up a little bit when I realized that not everyone is going to be happy for me.

Over the past few months, several of the former Cowboys greats have said some nice things about me. But that's because they're all believers too. If they know God, then they understand what I'm going through, and they're happy for me. The people who say the negative things aren't believers. Chances are those people wouldn't know God if He sat down on their doorstep. But they're the ones I'm praying for. And now they're also the ones I'm playing for.

Surrender

I feel now that, because of all that God has put me through, He must have been preparing me to go places that most people would never go, to speak to and touch some people in arenas that many might never see. God led me to a certain point, then He grabbed hold of me and turned me completely around in the most visible and eyeopening way, I believe, so that people would say, "Man, this is some kind of incredible conversion!" He's been preparing me to minister the Word. He allowed me to have succeess in almost everything I touched, and now I have absolutely no reason to doubt that He who has began a good work in me will be faithful to complete it in Christ.

Read, study, learn, that's all I do, because it's a high calling. That's why it was really tearing me up for so many years, being in circumstances like that where I knew, *Oh, my goodness, I've got to come on home.* But then I never wanted to be a hypocrite. I've always been honest and straightforward in everything I've done, and I never wanted to be any other way. I didn't want to have one foot in this camp and one foot in that one over there; I said I wasn't going to be like that. If I was ever going to get right with God and let Him take control of my life, then I was going to do it all the way, and I just wasn't ready to do it before that time.

I knew, more than anything, that I couldn't leave the women alone right then, so that's what prolonged it. But I made the cardinal mistake of trying to get myself together before I went to the Lord. You can't do that; you have to go to Him to get yourself together. So that was a mistake that prolonged it for a while. But finally I just surrendered. That was after I came to Dallas.

One of the main reasons I left San Francisco was because I was bored. No peace. I'm not a California type guy in the first place; but I was just bored. I got along with anybody, the fans, the employees, the janitors, the coaches, anybody and everybody, but some of the major figures on that team were down on me because I had that charisma and that attraction, that I could get along with everyone.

Everybody was cool with me, but I think that threatened some of the others around the team, as if I were stepping on their territory, so that was in the background I suppose. Anyway, it wasn't too long before I knew that I had to move on. I had a great year and a lot of success, but there was a lot of insecurity there.

When the Cowboys played at San Francisco in 1997, the media really played up the fact that I would be playing across from Jerry Rice, and that maybe there was some bad blood there. Jerry thought the press gave me too much credit for the 49ers' Super Bowl victory, and he had been quoted in the San Francisco *Examiner* as saying, "Can't no one individual win a Super Bowl!" He said, "We're very angry. Deion Sanders . . . it was like half the season when he came to this team. That's an insult to the guys who busted their butts . . . and were here all season."

He didn't stop there, of course, and he said some things about me that were way off base. Maybe it was his true feelings coming out, I don't know. If there was any bad blood between Jerry and me it was all one way because I was crazy about Jerry Rice. I mean, anybody can see he's a fantastic player, and I really thought he was cool. But he said some things and the press built it all up, and that's what created all the controversy. But I already knew I had to go somewhere else, and the Lord brought me to Dallas.

The reason I chose the Cowboys was very simple—dollars and cents! But when I made that decision, I didn't come to the highest bidder, even though everybody thought I did. The highest bidder was actually the Raiders. But something brought me to Dallas, and I think part of it was my relationship with Michael Irvin. I remember sitting in the hotel room after the baseball game, having a migraine headache, and I was just sitting there thinking, *Man, I've gotta make this decision about where I'm gonna go.* It was very stressful on me, wondering which way to turn. And I looked over at the tube and there was Jerry Jones in front of the microphone at a press conference saying, "I'm going to get Deion Sanders because he belongs with the Dallas Cowboys. I like Deion and I want him playing here with our team."

I said, "That's cool. I want to go there too." So I started calling Mike Irvin and we'd talk, and I was just feeling him out about the characteristics of the various guys on the team. I told him, "I've been to Atlanta and San Francisco, and I don't want to deal with any more jealousy or bitterness or envy. I don't want to deal with this mess. I just want to play ball and be left alone." And Mike was telling me about the fans in Dallas and what it's like to play here, and that's why I came.

Something Radical

Making the move to Dallas turned out to be a double blessing because Bishop Jakes had recently moved his ministry to Dallas from Charleston, West Virginia, about the same time. He moved his whole ministry and his national television base just like that, so God was putting me in position to make some dramatic changes in my life. And, of course, it was lucky for the Bishop that I was coming, too, because he didn't know a thing about football! Not a thing!

I'm so thankful because I had lost my stepfather the previous February and there was an emptiness in my life because of that. So it was a blessing that the Lord put Bishop Jakes into my life and since we've gotten to know each other he has helped fill that place in my heart that my fathers should have occupied. I had a hole in my life that needed filling, and God supplied just what I needed.

It was originally Carolyn's idea to go to the Potter's House for marriage counseling. We were trying to improve the relationship and she decided that we needed to go through counseling together. She knew she needed to take me to somebody she felt I would respect, somebody with a big enough ministry that I wouldn't feel there was some hidden agenda there.

It was funny how that came to pass, though. She had originally wanted to go to see another well-known pastor in Dallas, but he was out of town that week, involved in a big Promise Keepers rally, so instead of him she took me to meet Bishop Jakes.

I didn't want to be there, and he knew I didn't want to be there, so there was a little tension at first. After a little bit of that, though, I had enough and I told her I wasn't going to do that anymore. I couldn't sit there in the preacher's office and lie, and she was trying to put all the blame for our problems on me. Now, I admit that I had made a lot of mistakes and I was responsible for a lot of the unhappiness and disappointment she was feeling, but I wasn't the only one in the marriage, and I felt that we were about equally responsible for the breakup.

Most of the time I was basing my behavior on reaction; if you do this then I'm gone. We were constantly arguing about, "Who's the victim?" She would say she was the victim and I'd say, no, I'm the victim! Now that's a game all kinds of people play, and it's a dangerous game of self-delusion. But I didn't know that at the time. Bishop Jakes preached a powerful sermon on that topic about a year later—playing the blame game—so he knew what was going on there.

Anyway, I didn't want to be talking about all those personal things with some preacher; but I was a little surprised that this Bishop wasn't terribly impressed with me, either, or who I was. He didn't know anything about sports and, for that matter, he didn't even care; so that did get my attention. Later on we came to terms on that and he said that he would tell me about Jesus and about how I could get my life together if I would teach him something about football. That sounded like something I could handle, so I said, "You're on, Bishop!"

So he was very honest with me and, he will tell you, I was painfully honest with him. I came clean, and little by little I came to realize my desperate need for Jesus in my life. I was ready for something radical. Unfortunately, I don't think Carolyn was happy with what was happening and she eventually quit coming for counseling. She decided she had made a mistake and she said she didn't want anything to do with it any-more. But I was beginning to get a new idea of who I was in God's eyes, so I kept on coming back, kept on growing, kept on learning.

Carolyn moved to Houston to get on with her own life, without Deion Sanders. And now I've begun a new chapter in my own life as well.

chapter eleven

FIELD OF DREAMS

The real Deion Sanders has always had a strong work ethic and a strong desire to do the right thing. Even when I played for the Falcons I always used to talk to the guys about doing the right thing—not drinking, not smoking, staying straight, doing their best in practice, and always going to the higher expectancy level. They listened to me because I was doing it myself. I was doing it on the field and off.

It's not that I was religious or anything, but I always knew I needed a code of ethics, and I had a longtime habit of reading a verse of Scripture from the Bible every day. Even before I was delivered, I realized that there was something in that book that I needed to hear. Now if you had asked me an hour later what I had just read I probably wouldn't remember, because it wasn't in me. But my ex-wife, Carolyn, will tell you that every day I read a verse from the Bible.

It was a habit that goes back all my life, growing up, high school, college, all through the pros, baseball, football, I read at least one verse of Scripture every day. There was a time when I wouldn't play a game on Sunday in the NFL unless I was wearing my cross chain. Carolyn would be horrified if she forgot to give me my chain. We would have to send somebody back to the house to get my chain and bring it to me on the field.

I was so naive about spirituality at that time that I thought I had to play with the Lord around my neck, like I had Him on a chain! So I played every game with that chain hanging around my neck. But I always knew I needed a relationship with God. My mother and grandmother made sure I understood that I needed God in my life. But I wasn't living it. I just didn't know how to make the move to the next level.

My relationships with coaches, owners, and all the other people in professional sports organizations was demanding and challenging at times. I had to work with a lot of different personalities in baseball, football, and on the business side. But as a result I've had a chance to see a side of people that the public rarely gets to know.

Jerry Jones, the owner of the Dallas Cowboys, is one of the most caring, loving, respectful, and smart people I've ever known. Contrary to the way he's caricatured by the media, Jerry is a fine person and somebody I've really come to admire and respect. When he saw he needed a cornerback after Kevin Williams broke his ankle, he didn't waste any time signing me. I know there were a lot of pros and cons in the media back in 1995 and '96 when all that was going on, but Jerry Jones grabbed me the minute it became clear that I was ready to leave San Francisco and make a move.

Jerry knows business, and he knew that his team had just won two Super Bowls and all of a sudden they didn't win a third. I made the move from Atlanta to San Francisco in 1995, and the 49ers won the Super Bowl the year I was there. I'm not saying it was all because of me but everybody realized I brought something to the 49ers that they needed. So if you want to win a Super Bowl and you're smart enough to take that ingredient away from your chief competitor, then you still have the same team that won it for you a year ago. You take the edge away from your rival, and the result is that you win the Super Bowl the very next year.

Jerry Jones should have looked like one of the smartest men in the world but the media and some of the Dallas fans took that away from him because they didn't want to give him the credit he deserved.

If I gave away hundreds of millions of dollars, I'd want to know everything my team does too. That's all he does. Jerry is a hands-on owner. Dallas fans got used to the Clint Murchison hands-off approach, but Jerry's not made that way. He's not the kind of owner who can spend $100 million on a football team and then just pretend it doesn't mean anything when his team's getting their butts kicked. There may be some owners out there who can pull that off, and just sit back and give all the responsibility to somebody else, but Jerry is a hands-on guy. That's his style, and obviously it's worked very well.

But I'll tell you something else: You can't find a guy on that team who would say a bad word about Jerry Jones. The media and the fans give him a hard time, but the people who work with him every day will never do that.

Previous owners said, "I'll give you the money, or I'll hire the best coaches we can find, but then I'm going to trust you to run the team the best way you know how." But that's not the way Jerry does it, and you can't argue with what he has accomplished. With the old-style management you had twelve division titles, five Super Bowl appearances, and two world championships in twenty-five years. Jerry Jones gave you three Super Bowl victories in ten years, which is more than you had in the whole history of the team up to that time. So who's winning? Jerry's team sells more products than any other team in sports and makes millions more than any other NFL franchise.

I mean, what am I missing?

The NFL gives him a hard time, the fans give him a hard time, and all he does is win. They gave Jerry lip for signing with Nike, then the next year the whole NFL signed with Nike. Come on, man, this guy is an innovator! He is a blessing to the NFL. You'll never hear players talking Jerry down. Whenever we need somebody in a skill position on this team, Jerry will come around to the key players and say, "What do you think about this player or that guy over there?" He wants our input, and he wants to know what we think about the players who might be available.

Jerry went to Michael Irvin, Emmitt Smith, Troy Aikman, and the other captains on the team before he ever brought me in, and he asked each one of them what they thought about bringing Deion Sanders to Dallas. I know that for a fact. They all told him what they thought about it, then in the end Jerry did what he thought was best for the team. He made me an offer I couldn't refuse and brought me to Dallas.

Where Credit's Due

Another hot potato around Dallas and the league for a couple of years was all the controversy about losing Jimmy Johnson and bringing Barry

Switzer in to coach the team. I can't speak to all of that because I wasn't in Dallas at that time and I never played a day for Jimmy Johnson. But I loved Barry Switzer. He was a good man, too. There were never more than a couple of guys on the whole team who had anything against Barry.

If Barry was such a lousy coach, as the media kept saying, then why didn't the coaches ever say anything bad about him? You never heard any of the black players say anything bad about him, because he got along.

A lot of us defended him openly, in print, on TV, and many other ways. Some of the fans were heated up about that, saying, "Michael, come on! Why are you defending this guy?!" But Michael knew that Barry was just doing the job he was hired to do, and winning games every week. In fact, I said this in a press conference after we whipped the Washington Redskins back in November of 1997. I said, "Okay, man, we played a great game, we won, so let's give Barry the credit he deserves. Barry coached a great game."

One of the reporters stuck a microphone in my face and said, "Why give Barry the credit? What did he do?" and I said, "Look, man, you give it to him when we lose, so how about giving him a little credit when we win?"

About the only serious criticism came from Darrell Johnston and Troy Aikman, but it was never malicious or bitter in any way. Troy had played for Barry at Oklahoma when he first came out of high school. Barry was used to a running offense and Troy's skills were primarily in throwing the ball. Troy left Oklahoma and went to UCLA, and that was an outstanding choice, but that situation was always in the background. Darrell Johnston is close to Troy and I think they both felt that Barry didn't really understand Troy's game. But, with very few exceptions, most of that was kept pretty much under wraps.

Barry got along with everybody—well almost everybody—and he didn't do nothing to deserve the harassment he got from the fans. If Barry had won just one more game in San Francisco—when I was playing for the 49ers—then he would have won two Super Bowls back-to-back and been a national hero. Now that sounds like a heck of a coach to me; but whenever anybody wanted to find a scapegoat for their frustrations, they just automatically looked at Barry.

Shortly after the end of the 1997 season, Jerry let Barry go and brought on Chan Gailey from the Pittsburgh Steelers, and that's looking like one more coup for Jerry Jones. Coach Gailey said on TV a few weeks after coming to Dallas that this Cowboys team could go all the way first time out. A lot of people thought that sounded a little brash, and some of the media made comments about that. But was it really? Was he exaggerating?

Look at it from Coach Gailey's perspective. He just came here from the Steelers. The year they played Dallas in the Super Bowl they had Neil O'Donnell as their starting quarterback. Now, Neil is a fine player, but he's no Troy Aikman. The next year they had Kordell Stewart. He's a great athlete and a total player, but he's no Troy Aikman either. Besides that, Coach Gailey has never had players of the caliber of a Larry Allen, a Nate Newton, or an Erik Williams. No wonder he's upbeat!

With the veteran talent on this team, and with the outstanding new players picked up in the off-season through the draft and free agency, there should be nothing stopping this team from going all the way. Just imagine what the coach must be thinking: When Gailey walked out of that first team meeting, when he got to Dallas and had a chance to meet his players and get a good look at the talent he had to work with, don't you know he must have just been shaking his head in disbelief! He was saying, "I just walked out of a room full of future hall-of-famers!"

Dallas already has the second highest rated defense in the NFL, and all the offense needs to do is turn it up a little. I can see why this new coach is excited about being here. He has been taking his team to the play-offs and the division championship games every year with a coaching staff and players with a lot less talent than he's got with this team. Look at the guns he's got: Michael Irvin, Emmitt Smith, Troy Aikman, plus at least another dozen players who are all Pro-Bowl caliber.

So, no, I don't think it's bragging to say this team could go all the way in year one. He knows his track record and his abilities to run an offense, and he's walking in with a defense that's at the top of their game. So I can understand that.

The chemistry so far between the coaches and the team has been excellent. We have the same defensive coaches we had in 1997, and I think the offensive group has really come together very well. Sure, there are different styles, different ways of dealing with situations, and there are some things that we'll be doing in new or different ways in the future. But I really don't think you will notice much change in the look and feel of the Dallas Cowboys under Coach Gailey's command. Except that you're going to see some bigger numbers in the "W" column and a little more excitement when we play.

But I come back to this because I don't want to just blow past it. I've always been a Barry Switzer fan. I'm sorry. Not taking anything away from Coach Gailey, but I would never say anything against Barry and, personally, I wish he were still here. I love this new coach and I have no doubt he's going to do an outstanding job, but the fans and the media need to understand that it's not the coaches who win football games. It's the players.

More than that, though, something changed in the spirit of the guys when the season started going south. I think if you want to analyze a season you need to look at things individually, because if each player does his job and contributes his best effort individually, then the team will do just fine and you'll win most of your games. If you want to judge a season, don't just say, "Oh, the team did this and the team did that." You need to look at each player individually and examine how they contributed in key situations in key games.

Look at the performance of each offensive player and ask, "Is he playing as well as he played two years ago?" Or you might ask, "Is he playing consistently each week during the season?" Then look at each player on the defense and make your evaluation like that, one by one. Don't think you can make some sort of voodoo diagnosis of a team as a whole without taking it to the level of the individual player. That simply can't be done.

A lot of people have tried to put the blame for the Cowboys' problems on Emmitt Smith because he's had some games where he didn't perform up to his own standards. But you can't do that either. No one player can stop a championship team, just as no one player can win all by himself.

A Real Power Trip

Coaches can help set the pattern. They can help you get momentum and a sense of purpose and discipline in your game. But coaches don't win and lose games. Players do. If you're a professional athlete of the caliber to make it in the NFL, then nobody can help you do what only you can do. And you're dealing with grown men here. Ain't no coach that can fire me up and tell me to go out there and bust my butt if it ain't in me.

We've got twelve or thirteen Pro-Bowl players on our team. If every one of those guys plays like he's capable of playing, the Cowboys will do all right. Some of the problems this team has experienced go back to the personal lives of the players.

I know a lot of people said there seemed to be some kind of break-down, not just in the character of certain players but maybe in the level of expectations that management has concerning the personal lives of players. There's no question that the Cowboys became a sort of joke around the league for a while, and everybody—not just the media—was talking about the Cowboys as if we were all a bunch of outlaws.

I suppose that's where I came in. Power, money, and sex. It's something we deal with every day in the NFL. Visibility, praise, success, all those things go to a man's head if you're not well grounded, and that's what led to my own situation. Was it when I started getting all those endorsements and seeing myself on TV, having people throwing money at me everywhere I went? Was it something, maybe, that started back in grade school and junior high? Yes. Probably. All of the above.

Power comes when you're still just a kid and you find out you're gifted at something. When you discover you can do things that other kids can't do at that age, suddenly you realize you've got power. You do what you enjoy doing, you work at your game, and you begin to see that you're not just average, you're above average. You're above the norm. And that does something to your head.

Maybe you're the same age as the kid next to you, but you're doing things with your own style and flair that he can't do. You're doing stuff that people have never seen before. That was me. That's the awakening I experienced when I was six, seven, eight years old. I've never been a copier; I've always been an innovator and it worked for me and I've been very successful because of that. Being successful and competent gives you such power. But you've got to know how to handle it.

All the way through school I had power. It involved an attitude of self-confidence but I especially noticed the effect that it had on other people. I had enough power in high school that if I had ever said, "Okay, we're going to all skip school today," I would have been able to persuade a lot of people—not just the football and baseball teams, but the whole school. The athletic and the academically inclined people as well.

Even playing three sports I was able to hold on to a 3.0 grade point average all the way through school, and I was very knowledgeable about life. I never tried to get people to walk out of school, of course, but I knew I could. I knew I had that much power. If I didn't feel like practicing, nobody else would practice either; but if I felt like working twice as hard, then everybody would go along and they'd work hard, too.

I always had good instincts, not just on the football field but I always seemed to have an innate sense about wanting to do the right thing. Now and then I would run into guys who had the instincts and the talent, but they used their power in the wrong way. In fact, on the album I made in 1993 I did a rap song talking about my hometown.

I said, "I stayed right; they took a left." I think everybody in sports has stories about guys who were more talented than they were, but somewhere along the way they took a left and got involved in stuff that ate them up. They wanted it the quick way and I was willing to wait. That's why we have drug dealers: people don't want to wait. That's why we have casinos: people don't want to earn their money, they want it now. Instant gratification.

By the time I finished college and started my career in the pros I was beginning to see how people used their power in an all new way. Suddenly I had the power to attract people because of my skills as a player. I was quick on my feet and because I had charm and charisma and was quick with my tongue, I could get things.

People who know me know that, at heart, I'm a comedian, always clowning around and joking with my homeys. You see some players who try to do that, but they can't quite pull it off, and they get their cleats in their mouth, so to speak! But I've been blessed with quick wit and a good sense of humor, and you know that's a kind of power in itself. I also talk about some of that on that rap album that not many people bought!

Right now I have a lot of power, and it includes both the power to destroy and the power to heal. I realize that even a small mishap or mistake could damage a lot of people right now. Being in the wrong place at the wrong time, being with the wrong person, or if a woman were to make a false accusation about me it could destroy a lot of people I care about. It doesn't have to be true, just a false accusation can damage you when you're trying to show that you're a new creature in Christ and trying to walk in a new direction.

Where I'm headed, and where the Lord is taking me, that would be a very serious thing and, as you know, I don't even let myself get into those kinds of compromising situations. I don't like to go anywhere by myself. You can go places and do things with your power, but using it incorrectly can destroy you. There are guys I've played with who have done all those things and some of them have lost control and gone over the edge because of it.

Those three things often, if not always, come together: power breeds money, and if you have those you can have sex. Unrestrained power has unlimited appeal and persuasion, so it's not accidental that those three things which most people desire should be attached to each other.

You see, money just allows you to become who you really are. The more money you have, the freer you are to be who you are inside. If you're a giving person by nature, then with money you will be more generous. If you're an acquisitive and stingy person, then you'll be even worse if you have control of a lot of money. Money magnifies your personality and enhances who you are inside.

When you give somebody a lot of money, it's like pushing fast-forward on the VCR: You're going to find out who that person is real quick. You're also going to get a new view of the people around you. You'll find out who they are—no doubt about that. That's what it does. Using money incorrectly can destroy you just as much as using power incorrectly.

But if you have money without a proper focus, you'll never be satisfied. I found that out, and whenever I give my testimony I tell people what I discovered in my own life. If you have five dollars you want six; if you have ten you want twenty. That's just human nature. So no matter how much money you have, you're never satisfied. You always want more than you've got.

More money, more money, more money! That's why the people on Wall Street are going crazy all the time. All they think about day and night is how they can get more money. When are you going to be satisfied with what you have? The answer is never. Unless you have God in your life, and unless He gives you the capacity to put it in proper perspective, you will never find peace with money. First you've got to have peace with God, and then with yourself.

Money can heal if used correctly, but if it's used carelessly and without proper understanding it can destroy friendships, marriages, and all your other relationships. People who exploit money and who allow money to use them never know who their friends are, and whenever anyone is nice to them, they think, *What's your motive? What are you after?* And if you're not careful you'll get a lot of people hanging on you, trying to hang around because they want what you've got. What kind of life is that?

Once I began my walk and started coming closer to the Lord, I realized that those three things—power, money, and sex—are very powerful and that they have two sides. I had seen one side up to that point. Now I needed to see the other side. God was doing a work in my life, and He was just about to turn on the Light.

chapter twelve

MY SOURCE OF STRENGTH

P ower, money, sex. They're such powerful urges in most people. Some people spend their whole lives thinking that if they could just get more power, money, and sex, they would be happy. But as somebody who has had more than my share of all three, I can tell you this: In themselves, those things will not make you happy. It's okay to have them, but if they're not put into proper perspective, and if they're not used with appropriate balance and restraint, they can kill you.

What do those words say to you? Power, money, sex. That's a pretty good description of the world we live in today. Just look at the magazine racks in the airport, or the bookstore shelves, or listen to the things people are talking about on the job or at the club. Power, money, sex. It seems like that's all anybody wants to think about or talk about anymore.

Take a look at what's happened to daytime TV! Shows like Springer, Oprah, Montel, Howard Stern, the soaps, and even the six o'clock news are knee-deep in stuff you don't even want your kids to know about. Or look at what's been going on in Washington the last five years. You talk about power, money, and sex. What else is it?!

But I know all those things on a first-name basis, and I can tell you this: Those things can blind you to other things that are a lot more important to your success and your happiness in life. My experience, including my nearly fatal collision with doubt, emptiness, and disillusionment, was dramatic, even if it's not all that uncommon anymore. But all over the world people are discovering what I discovered on that roadside along the Ohio River. You've got everything your mind can conceive of. You're holding all the toys the world has told you that you've got to have if you want to be happy. But you're desperately hungry, empty, and you're just dying inside.

I found out that you can be lying in the bed with three beautiful women and that won't be enough. You can have millions of dollars in the bank and carry enough cash to buy you anything your mind can imagine, and it won't be enough. You can walk into any restaurant in town and they put your name up at the top of the list. Or people can come up to you and call you Sir, and ask for your autograph, and everybody is wanting to be around you all the time, but that won't be enough.

When you grow up, a young black kid like I was, and everybody starts talking about you, calling you Mr. Sanders, and telling you how good you are, man, that can go to your head. Pretty soon you start to think you are somebody. But you're nobody until you've got a greater purpose in your life, and I found out you can never have that kind of purpose until you know God. I learned my lesson the hard way. Unfortunately, some people will go through hell before they realize that's the truth.

A lot of people dream of possessing what I have—fame, fortune, athletic talent. They believe those things could satisfy them. Millions of people spend more than they can afford playing the lottery every day, thinking that if they just had a lot of money they could solve all their problems. But why doesn't it? Whenever you read about lottery winners in the papers, they only show you the smiling, happy faces. They never show you what really happens after that.

You'll never see the follow-up stories about lottery winners. Why? Because then you would see that, in nine cases out of ten, all that money destroys people's lives. People see what's on the outside, and guys like myself make it look so wonderful and so desirable, and the average person doesn't even realize that it's all just a facade. It's a mirage, a myth we created, while on the inside we may be torn apart and dying of emotional starvation.

I sometimes think of it like an actor coming onto the set in some ratty old studio. His life may be terrible, and everything around him in his real life is filthy and dirty, but he comes out into the lights and somebody says, "Action!" What the public sees is all smiles and enthusiasm and happiness, but then, when the lights go off, it's just another broken-down person who spends every waking hour in a living hell.

What do you do when you look up into the stands and see sixty or seventy thousand people yelling and cheering because they came to watch you play? And you have the big dinner after the game and everybody's patting you on the back and talking about how great you are. Later you get off by yourself and you look into the mirror and you see the soul of a lonely, hurting, broken little child, and you know that all that celebration and excitement is just noise and it doesn't mean anything. Inside, you're empty. You can be surrounded by thousands, even millions, of people, and you're empty and alone.

You can spend ten years of your life in a relationship with a woman and still be lonely. Then who are you going to cry to? You were there for your wife and family to cry on. You were there for your children and your parents to cry on because you supported them. You were there for your friends to lean on. But who is there for you? No one. Because no one knows what you're feeling inside.

They don't even know who you are because you've been perpetrating a fraud. You've been living a lie for so many years and they don't even know you. For a wife to lie in the same bed with you for nine years and think she's done such a tremendous job, being a wife and mother and doing all the things someone in her position should do, and all that time she doesn't even know you. But that's what happens when God is not in it.

Other People's Mistakes

I wasn't raised badly. My mother had strict requirements for me and she wouldn't take any lip from me or anybody else. I was exposed to some things I didn't like and that I regret, except that being exposed to those things made me realize I didn't want anything to do with them. Being exposed to alcoholism caused me never to drink. Being exposed to drugs caused me to stay away from drugs. That was my reaction. Now, I don't recommend that for everyone, but for whatever reasons the things I saw my two fathers do when I was a child made me want to avoid those destructive behaviors by any and all means.

Now my kids aren't going to be exposed to those things because they might not be as strong as I was. I grew up very fast and, as I've said before, I felt like I became the adult in my household at an early age, and I'm thankful that my circumstances gave me that kind of maturity. But I'm going to do everything I can to see that my own children receive a godly upbringing and learn godly values at home and in all aspects of their lives.

From time to time people will tell me that I'm a role model for their kids. But that disturbs me. I don't think moms and dads should encourage their young people to look up to athletes and celebrities as role models. I don't even like the term *role model* because that's exactly what it is: a model playing a role. Chances are, your child is only going to see me for three hours on a Sunday afternoon, or in some commercial or endorsement I might do on TV. He may see me doing some interview after the game, or hear something I've said on a radio show, but I'm not going to be there to take him to school or to help him with his homework.

I'm not going to provide for him or teach him right from wrong. That's a job only his own parents can do. I recognize that I have a responsibility, not only to baseball and football fans around the country but to the Lord, and that I am to say and do things that young people will see and admire and try to emulate. But my first responsibility is to my own kids. So I try to put everything in its proper perspective.

It goes like this: My first responsibility is to God. I should be the person I need to be for my relationship with my heavenly Father. After that, I should be there for my family, to provide for them and love them and nurture them as the gifts from God that they truly are. My third priority is my ministry and my career, on the football field or the baseball diamond, and doing all the various things that I have to do to pursue this occupation to the best of my ability. And only then, somewhere down the list, is my responsibility to be a good example for your kids.

Think about it. What happens when a role model fails you and does something destructive? What happens when a man your kids admire gets caught with drugs or with another man's wife? What happens when someone like the president gets caught in a sordid relationship? What do your kids think when they see stars and celebrities acting like idiots and throwing money around and living as if their personal pleasure is the only thing that matters? Is that what you want them to learn? Are those values that will help them succeed in life and become mature and responsible adults? I don't think so.

Personally, I don't like parents putting that burden on me. Just because God has given me a talent that I've been able to use in such a way that it has brought me success and prosperity, that's not enough reason for your child to admire and imitate me.

I teach in the high schools in Dallas, and I hear of kids blaming their bad behavior on "peer pressure." Where does that come from? They blame their behavior on peer pressure because they want to fit in. They want to be "somebody." They want to fit in with the crowd. They want to be acknowledged. Therefore, if they can be acknowledged by doing bad things, then that's what they do.

It's like me going across the bridge that day with my football buddies in high school, when they were smoking pot on the way home. I could have given in, avoided the embarrassment, and done the easy thing and smoked pot with them. I mean, I thought about it. There was a voice that said, "Sure, you can go along with that." But I had good home training, and there was another voice in me that said, "No way, man. That would be wrong. And besides, your mama will kill you!" And that's what made up my mind.

It sure wasn't some role model. I wasn't saying, "Hey, man, I wonder what Hank Aaron or O. J. or Muhammad Ali would do right now?" I didn't even think about that! I was thinking, *Man, my mama gonna tear my behind when I get home if I come in smellin' like I been around somebody smoking weed!* And that's when I told them, "Hey, man, stop the truck and put me in the back."

Parents have such a tremendous privilege and responsibility to raise their kids the right way. For me, being a daddy is my favorite job. I thought I was a wonderful daddy until I came to Christ and found out what fatherly love is really all about! The Bible says, "Train up a child in the way he should go, and when he is old he will not depart from it." I want to train up my children the way God would have me raise them, to train them up spiritually. I want to train my daughter, Deiondra, to be the best young woman and someday the best adult she can possibly be. I want to train her and Deion Luwynn to be Christians, to be good people, to have good hearts, to exhibit the fruits of the Spirit in their lives and to be filled with the Holy Ghost when they're ready for that step. I want them to know the love of Jesus and the love of God.

It's such a joy for me as their father to hear them recite Bible verses and to say their prayers. They sing Bible songs when we're in the car and we pray together. And when they're away with their mother they will send me beautiful little notes that say, "Daddy, I love you and I'm praying for you." When they go to bed at night, I give them my blessing and lay hands on them as they go to sleep.

They go to church every Sunday, and when they're here I help Deion with his little suit and Deiondra with her dresses. I do all that as a daddy because I'm playing both roles. I have to be as tender as a mother and at the same time as tough and reliable as a father. I get to spend a lot of time with them in the off-season and I have them all summer, so that's very special for me, and I don't want to let those precious times get away from me.

I love being with my kids, and I love doing things with them. I've always loved to fish, so I took them with me and taught them how to fish and now they love it too. And they really love tennis. I love to just play with them around the house, to be the pony, to jump with them on the trampoline in the backyard. They love to swim. They crawl up on Daddy's back and play in the pool. And they really love for me to take them to places like Discovery Zone, Fun Fest, Malibu Raceway, or Chuck E. Cheese.

So my favorite things to do with them are, first, to go fishing, and second, to take them shopping for new clothes. For some reason those two things give me a real sense of relationship with them. Helping my son choose his clothes is easier, of course, since I have a pretty good idea what boys like to wear. My daughter is another challenge, but I love doing that and taking her shopping just as much. But you know we go out in the yard and play ball together and play in the swimming pool.

I like to take them shopping, but most of the time we don't go to the mall. We just go to some department store. But both kids are jealous of our private time and if anybody comes up to get an autograph or something like that, they'll say, "No, he doesn't do that when he's with us. He's just daddy!" And they'll tell you quick: "Daddy does not sign autographs when he's with us!"

Both Deiondra and Deion Luwynn love sports, but most of all they just love for us to be together. Deiondra is into gymnastics and Bucky loves all sports—football, baseball, basketball—and he loves going to work with me. When we're practicing, he'll be on the sidelines with his little uniform on. After practice he comes over and takes off his uniform like I do, then he puts on his little shower shoes and we go in and shower, then we get dressed and go home. And he loves to dress like Daddy, too, in pin-striped suits with flashy buttons!

I didn't have that kind of relationship with my father, but now that I know how important it is for dads and their children to know each other, to love each other, and to spend time together, I'm taking every opportunity to be with my kids and show them how much I really care for them. Because that's part of my calling, too.

By the Grace of God

The most positive aspect of all the success I've had, I suppose, is the respect that comes with having position and influence. But the bad part is that when you become a public person, and when you've got a lot of influence, you can never relax. You're afraid all the time. You get to the place where you feel like you've got to have four heads, looking in all directions, because you're always worried about somebody using you and manipulating you. You always doubt their motives.

Everybody wants a piece of you, and if you're not walking with the Lord you have no discernment and no way to separate the good ones from the bad ones. When I give my testimony, I frequently say that people come into your life for three purposes: some for a reason, some for a season, and some forever. It's up to you to distinguish who those people are and what they're coming for, because everyone in your life is there for one of those purposes. And in the end, only God can give you the discernment to tell one from the other.

A lot of people—including some Cowboys fans and sports fans in general—would like for that they call "This Christian Thing" in my life to fail. They don't believe it's real, or they don't want it to be real. They like the old Deion; he's flashier, more outrageous and unrestrained, the way they'd like to be. Ever since I became a Christian, sportswriters and some of the more skeptical fans have been watching me like a hawk, and some of them have even gone to the point of purposely putting obstacles, pressures, and certain temptations in my way to see if I would let down.

But I had pressures when I was in the world, and I don't really think this is any different. When I see it, I realize how powerful the Lord is and what a threat to Satan's kingdom the Christian faith must be because so many of Satan's people are working overtime trying to destroy it. Christ is in me and He is my source of strength. I don't have to worry anymore about who I am, because, as Paul says, "I can do all things through Christ who strengthens me" (Phil. 4:13).

You know, if I had come out as a Buddhist or a Muslim or as a follower of any other religion in the world, nobody would have said a thing. But when I take a stand for Jesus Christ, some people just go crazy. But the only reason is because they don't believe. They don't want what I have to be true, because if it's true they'll have to admit that their own lives are all messed up and they need to make some changes.

This is why power, money, and sex are so dangerous. Not just in having those things, but in believing that you have to keep seeking and grasping for them. Those who are living by this world's values believe that if only they could have all the things that I have, then they would be happy and prosperous, too! They think the answer is in more power, more money, and more sex. But that's not it.

Today I'm learning not to put myself into situations where I can be diverted from my desire to serve God. One of the things I discovered after I came to faith was that I had been attracting what I was. When I was in the world and going to the clubs, I attracted the kind of women who liked to party and have a good time like I did.

When I was in the world I attracted who I was. It was always the fun, sexy, party people. Now I'm attracting people who love the Lord and recognize that God always comes first in my life. And that's what they want, too. When I go to dinner with a woman now, I put Matthew, Mark, Luke, and John right between us! And when we get through with all those books, we know how to Acts!

I understand that people have always wanted me to fail, but this is not something you can fail at. What if Deion Sanders made a mistake? It could happen. I'm human. I certainly do not plan to or want to let anything become a stumbling block in my life, but what if something like that did happen? God will be there for me. This is not a baseball game. Nobody is winning or losing here, and there's no big electronic scoreboard keeping a record of runs, hits, and errors. Deion Sanders is covered by the blood of Jesus now. He loves the Lord with all his heart. Only time will tell a lot of these people where I stand and what the Lord has done for me. But time will tell, and I'm in it for the marathon—not the sprint.

In the chapters that follow I want to look at some of the teachings of my mentor and teacher Bishop T. D. Jakes, because that will give you a good sense of what I've learned about power, money, and sex. This was something I really needed to hear, and I think a lot of people reading my story probably need to hear it as much as I did. Which brings me to something else I need to say. You see, this is not just my story. It's your story, too.

So many people who've achieved success know what I'm talking about. They've all had the same feelings in one way or another. They've been there. It's those who have never quite made it—never had power, never had money, never had the erotic adventures they think they deserve—who keep chasing the mirage and thinking that it's just a matter of time until they'll really be happy. Happiness is based entirely on circumstances and situations and those things can change on a moment's notice. That's why the Bible doesn't include happiness as one of the fruits of the spirit.

But, anyway, it's not true. I've been there, and I can tell you. It's not what you think it is. I had that stuff and I was your basic human crash dummy. Those things cannot make you happy; only God can ever satisfy the hunger inside of you. That's why I was on the back side of that desert for so long. Sometimes it's not until you're willing to try anything that you're ready for God in your life. And He may have to let you go through hell to bring you to your senses. But when you wake up, and when you're finally broken in your spirit, then He can bring miracles into your life and turn you completely around. That's what this story is really about.

PART III

chapter thirteen

A LESSON IN POWER

These next three chapters are some of the things I've learned from Bishop T.D. Jakes. As you will see, this is what Bishop has taught me about power, money, and sex, along with my own comments. You may think this is strange to include in my autobiography, but this is why I wrote the book in the first place. Because these teachings changed my life forever. They set me on the road to meet my Lord, and that's why I want to share them with you—maybe they'll change your life, too.

Without power, nothing worthwhile ever gets accomplished. That's one of the things that Bishop T. D. Jakes taught me. Everybody needs a power source. Everything needs a power source. The reason the light comes on when you walk into a room and flip on the switch is because there's a power source. If you take away the supply of power, the light can do nothing. It's useless. It has absolutely no power in and of itself. But men and women need power, too, and the only way they can have it is through a relationship with something or someone powerful.

If you're someone who understands nothing about relationships, you don't really have power. You may have some of the symbols of power and you may hide behind those things—whether it's money or sex or fame or however you want to define it—but you don't really have power until you're grounded in something that ignites you, fills you, and empowers you to go forward.

Some people have trouble keeping the lights on because they're not plugged in. They may have all the mechanical apparatus but if they're unplugged they've got none of the fire. They've got to have juice to function properly. You can have all the mechanical details, and you spend all your energy trying to prove to people that you have it, but you will never be powerful publicly until you're wired in and grounded privately.

Ultimately, of course, this means that you cannot talk about power without talking about God. Because God is the ultimate Power Source from which everything else emanates. God is the Supplier, the divine Power Utility, the ultimate Connection. Without Him, you'll always be unplugged and useless. But once you get hooked in to that Utility, the power will come on in your life and you'll begin to manifest new radiance and a beauty you've never known. And you'll become useful in a multiplicity of ways.

Now, as you're thinking about getting connected to this divine Power Source, I hope you won't think that this is just something for your personal magnetism and charm. Okay, that may come for some people. But what we're talking about here is a lot more important than that. God gives you power, not just being successful in life but, as Paul says, power to become the sons of God. He says, "For as many as are led by the Spirit of God, these are sons of God" (Rom. 8:14).

The apostle Johns says, "As many as received him, to them gave he the power to become the sons of God" (John 1:12 KJV). It may sound unbelievable, but it's true. If you're not hooked up to anything in your private life, then after a while your public life becomes barren and dead. But with God, you fuel up privately so that you can be powerful publicly. And then the power becomes transferable so that you can use it to become whatever you need to be.

You know, it's stressful to live a lie. It works you to death. That's what causes batteries to go dead, because they have no power beyond themselves. They can give off a little energy for a while and the light may shine momentarily, but before long things start to go dim because they're not hooked up to anything lasting. If you want to keep on burning, then you need to get plugged up to something bigger and stronger than you are.

A lot of people these days are like batteries on the verge of running down. They've got just enough juice to flicker and sputter for a while, and at times they may have just enough power to imitate the real thing, but after a while they begin to flicker and their energy just fades away. When that happens they start looking, searching, digging around—they've got to have something to build them back up.

"What's wrong with this woman?" they may ask. "She's not helping me. She's hindering me!" And they get angry and say, "How can you be with me and not help me? You said you were going to help me!" But if that's you talking, listen to me. You don't really understand what's happening. She's not your problem! She can't give you the power!

When your energy is depleted your first reaction is to start changing things: changing cars, changing jobs, changing neighborhoods, changing relationships, changing this and that, because you're desperate and looking for answers in all the wrong places. Before long you're trying things you said you would never try. You're reaching out to people you said you'd never be with. You're dialing those old phone numbers, replaying those old memories, and you're holding on to things you thought you would never touch because you're running out of power and you're desperate.

Through his counseling with men and women, Bishop has found that every man has got to have someplace he can go and fall apart. You need to have someplace where you can just go and say, "I'm at the end of my rope; I am running out of strength. I need to be refueled so I can be powerful publicly. I need someplace where I can go and strengthen myself so that when the trumpet blows I'll be ready for the next show."

The prophet Isaiah said that power comes from God. He says, "He gives power to the weak, and to those who have no might He increases strength. Even the youths shall faint and be weary, and the young men shall utterly fall, but those who wait on the LORD shall renew their strength; they shall mount up with wings like eagles, they shall run and not be weary, they shall walk and not faint" (Isa. 40:29–31).

God says, *I can give you back what you're losing. I can put back what life is taking out of you. But if you expect to be powerful publicly, you're going to have to be hooked up to Me.* Then He tells you that "those who wait on the LORD shall renew their strength" (Isa. 40:31). Now the word *wait* doesn't mean like sitting around with your hands in your lap wondering when

God's going to show up. It means "wait" like a waiter in a fine restaurant waiting on tables. It means to serve the Lord.

That tells us there is something about serving the Lord that gives us that special connection to power we're all looking for. That verse in Isaiah says, "Those who wait on the LORD shall renew their strength; they shall mount up with wings like eagles, they shall run . . ." You've still got to run, but you don't run out of strength. You shall "run and not be weary." You shall "walk and not faint," because you will be serving the Lord, and He's got all the power in Himself.

Running with Endurance

As an athlete and speaker, I travel all the time. So when Bishop speaks of his busy schedule, I know just what he means.

> Whenever I look at my schedule, I can't even figure out how I do all the things I have to do in a day. There is no physical way a man could keep a schedule like mine, doing all the things I have to do, and going all the places I have to go, by natural means. Only God's empowerment allows me to do it.
>
> People sometimes come up to me and they say, "I don't understand how you do all you do, Bishop! You must really be strong!"
>
> But I say, "Oh, no! I'm not strong. I'm plugged! I'm hooked up! I'm connected!"
>
> So let me ask you: What are you plugged into?

This is really important. If you fool around and plug into something that has no power, no wonder your lights won't come on. Are you trying to plug into your charm and good looks? That won't do it. Are you trying to plug into money? That won't do it. Are you trying to plug into sex? Or maybe your job? Sure, go ahead, and someday they'll drop you like a hot potato. Or maybe you're plugged into your body and you're all built up and hard; but what's going to happen to you when you get sick? What's going to give you power then?

Suppose you have a car wreck and suppose you're left a paraplegic. Suppose you end up in a wheelchair. How can you plug into something that could change without notice? You plug into God and He don't ever change. Your honey might get funny, but God don't change. Your money might be funny, but God don't change. Your job might fire you, but God don't change. Please! You better plug into something that don't have no dry cells in the battery!

God wants to hook you up so that you can be a man of power. He wants you to have power, but it has to come from appropriate places. He just wants to deliver you from imitations of life. God doesn't mind you having things. He minds things having you. God is flamboyant. He decorated heaven. Heaven is dressed up! Anybody who designs their house and puts gold on the floor is flamboyant! Anybody who's got gates of pearl is flamboyant! God designed the priestly outfit described in Exodus chapter 28 and He put jewels all over the breast of the garment. He had twelve stones in rows up and down the front.

Moses describes this garment with three rows of jewels containing sardius, topaz, emerald, turquoise, sapphire, diamond, agate, and amethyst, and a fourth row of beryl, onyx, and jasper. The coat was blue, with garments of white, and he had other elements of crimson, plus a hat on his head. And all these jewels were set in solid gold settings (Ex. 28:17–20). You talk about Deion Sanders or T.D. Jakes being flamboyant! God didn't give his people a pair of blue jeans, tennis shoes, and a T-shirt and say, "That's all I want you to have!" So hear what's happening here. God doesn't mind you having things; rather, He minds things having you.

God will bless you the day He can trust you. If He can't trust you, you'll get so caught up in the things He gave you that you'll forget who gave them to you. Isn't that right? Just breathe in. Take a deep breath. Who do you think gave you that breath? If He didn't let you, you couldn't catch your breath. If God didn't love you and help you, you couldn't take one more breath of air.

I have learned so much in my weekly visits to a local home for the elderly; it has changed my views on a lot of things. This is something Bishop Jakes addresses when he says that some of us need to go down to the hospital and visit some people who can't catch their breath. Oxygen all around them and they can't catch a breath. Can you imagine what that must feel like? Think about it and maybe you'll start to realize how dependent we are on God's good gifts. Go ahead and write a check for breath! Seduce you some oxygen! I don't know whether you serve Him or not but sooner or later you're going to need Him. Because God is the giver of all good gifts.

The apostle James says, "Every good gift and every perfect gift is from above, and comes down from the Father of lights, with whom there is no variation or shadow of turning" (James 1:17). Do you really think you can live without that? Do you even want to try? This is the God who is the Lover of your soul. This is your Power Source.

God never asks you to do anything without giving you something. He would never ask something of you if He hadn't given it to you, because the truth is you can't give God anything that He hasn't already given to you. Whenever God asks you something it's a compliment, because He would never ask you for it if He hadn't already given it to you. What can you give God that He didn't give you?

The book of Genesis tells us how God touched Adam and Eve in the Garden, and through them He blessed all mankind forevermore. It says, "God blessed them, and God said to them, 'Be fruitful and multiply; fill the earth and subdue it' (Gen. 1:28). He told them to "have dominion." First, He said "multiply", second, "multiply," third, "fill the earth," fourth, "subdue it," and finally, "have dominion." Five things. Those are the commandments of God. But God had already made provision and empowered the man and the woman to carry out His commands.

But the Bible also says that, a man "who has no rule over his own spirit is like a city broken down, without walls" (Prov. 25:28). It means you have no protection, you have no defense. You have no spiritual immunity. I call it spiritual AIDS. We tend to be afraid of people with AIDS, but the truth is, they ought to be afraid of us. Because little diseases that we carry around that don't even slow us down can be fatal to them. Their immune system is so weakened by their disease that, unless we sleep with them or have some sort of intimate contact with them, we're more of a danger to them than they are to us.

God said if you cannot control your own spirit, you have no immunity. So whatever comes by you, you catch it. And whoever comes by you, you catch it. And because you have no walls, anything goes. This is the word *lascivious*. It means you give in to unrestrained action, unrestricted lust and desire. You can't help yourself. You'll do something and you may feel bad about it later and say, "How come I'm like that?" The Bible says it's because you haven't ruled your own spirit.

So what's the first thing I need to do to get on-line with God's power supply? I need to conquer myself. I need to subdue me and bring myself up under control. Then after I bring myself up under control I have to have dominion over me. I have to set up reign. I have to know when to tell myself, *No, that's far enough. Stop right there!*

Plugging In

Whether you're talking about lust or temper or anything else that's troubling your life and emotions, you have to trust God for the strength to get back in charge. You can't fight your way back. You can't do it in bitterness. Do you know that the Bible says, "For the wrath of man worketh not the righteousness of God"? (James 1:20 KJV). That means you're never going to get to a right place in an angry way. It means you're not going to beat your wife into a good marriage. The righteousness of God only works in the hearts of men and women who have subdued their lustful natures and come into submission to their higher natures and placed their faith in Jesus Christ. And that's where the real power begins.

If you want to be somebody, then you need to be connected to Somebody, and that Somebody is the Lord Jesus Christ who said, "All power is given unto me in heaven and in earth" (Matt. 28:18 KJV). As soon as you get the power flowing, you will see incredible changes taking place in your life. But until you plug in, it just won't happen. You can't use a tape recorder if it's not plugged up. Maybe you've been living your entire life and never been plugged up. Maybe you are wondering why you're even here and you don't know the answer.

At many points in his lessons, Bishop Jakes touches on some of the deepest areas of our lives. He asks, for example, haven't you ever wondered why you weren't a stillborn? Haven't you ever wondered why you weren't aborted? Why you didn't die a crib death? Why you did crazy stuff and still survived? Haven't you ever thought about why you made it out of that car wreck? Why you haven't lost your mind? Don't you know that God kept you alive for a reason? You'll never know who you are until you get plugged into

God and find out your purpose and find out what He can do with your life!

It's only when you put away all of those symbols of success and temporary power and get hooked up to some real power that you can begin to find out why you're still here. You're not here because you're so smart. There are people smarter than you that are dead! You're not here because you're so gifted. There are people more gifted and more talented than you sleeping up under a bridge. I hate to hurt your feelings, but that's a fact.

For some time now Bishop Jakes has been ministering in the prisons, and I've begun to do some of that myself. In his series on power, money, and sex, Bishop makes the point that there are guys locked up down there for the rest of their lives who are better looking, stronger, more gifted than you are. And there's some of you that if it wasn't for God's mercy you'd be in there right now! So before you go thinking you've got it all together, and you're so smart, or that you're God's gift to the opposite sex, you'd better check your connections. What's your source, my friend? Do you know where your power is coming from? Do you really?

"From time to time," Bishop says, "I ask the men in our congregation at the Potter's House in Dallas to fill out questionnaires to help me get a better idea of the issues on their hearts, and one of the main things the men talk to me about is power in relationships. I appreciate it when they share their hearts with me because I don't want to be treating somebody's foot when it's their head that's messed up."

A lot of those questions say, "How do we get power in our relationships?" Some say, "How do I get my wife to respect me? How do I get her to appreciate me and validate me?" And there are several things that come into play with these issues. One of the first is that you've got to look at how you got into the situation you're in.

When teaching is real and true, it can also be very personal and painful. I feel that myself when Bishop teaches on the basic conflicts that happen when there is infidelity in a marriage. Some folks have done things that cause their mates to lose respect for them. Now, you can't walk in and beat on your chest and demand what you've already forfeited. You can't expect a wife to love a man who's been messing with some other woman or doing things behind her back and acting like it's okay because he deserves it! She's not buying any of that, and she's not going to give him the respect and appreciation he wants when he's been cheating and lying and going behind her back. She's just not made that way.

It takes time to rebuild trust if there has ever been infidelity in a relationship. And some of you need to realize that fact—particularly with women as it concerns adultery. You see, women define adultery as the epitome of betrayal. I think men have trouble understanding what that means to a woman. Outside of Christ, a man thinks he can sleep with Nellie, Ellie Mae, and Susybelle, and still say, "But my heart belongs to mama!" And if he gets caught cheating, or if Ellie Mae starts showing, the first thing he's going to say is, "But, honey, I love you!" And she's not buying it because she's not made that way!

Bishop observes that, biologically, men have this propensity to have their body in one place and their emotions in another. We don't tend to get vulnerable about the giving of flesh. But when you start fooling with our hearts, now you've got tears in my eyes. . . . But the same way men whimper about somebody breaking their heart and trifling with their emotions, that's how women feel when you take your body and share it with somebody else. And why shouldn't she feel that way! She has a right. You promised to be faithful, didn't you?

When you get serious about turning your life around, and when you finally come around and decide you want God to make things right in all your relationships, you have to face the fact that now there's a distrust issue that you'll have to deal with first. And you're going to have to pray and not fuss. You're going to have to pray and prove. Why pray? Because only God can heal. Pray, "God, help her to see that I'm not who I was." And stop trying to rush her through a healing process until you've convinced her that you are not who you were. And then give it some time.

Paul says in 1 Corinthians 11:3, "But I would have you know, that the head of every man is Christ; and the head of the woman is the man; and the head of Christ is God" (KJV). That's not my rule, it's God's rule, and that's the way He ordained it. But if any of that gets out of order, you've got a real mess. Jesus says that He is over you in responsibility and authority just like you are over her. But if you are not submitted to Him, He says,

"I'm going to show you what it means to love somebody who's disobedient and disrespectful!"

Planning Ahead

To have power, you've got to be connected. To have power in your life, you need a relationship with the Author of life. But having power affects all your relationships with other people as well. And once you understand what God is looking for in you, then you can begin to use the power He has given for daily living. It's like alternating current: God gives, you receive. He empowers, you respond. And, in turn, you gain the benefits of that relationship every day of your life, as long as you're walking and talking with Him.

Bishop tells about reading an amazing thing in the paper a few months ago, an article that really got his attention. It was a story about Congressman Joe Kennedy, one of the young members of the Kennedy clan up in Massachusetts, who decided not to run for governor of the state. What struck me was that the story said that there's never been a Kennedy who ran for the office of governor of Massachusetts who didn't win. That's amazing. But do you know why? Because each generation of Kennedys taught the next generation of Kennedys how to function in politics.

All of us—black, white, and brown—wrestle with problems in this area, but Bishop teaches that there are some areas where black Americans have some unique concerns. "I'm convinced," he says, "that one of the major problems for African-Americans today is that we have been fighting a number of generational curses that come from our experience of slavery and the way that has worked its way down through our culture. The Bible says that the sins of the fathers are passed down to the third and fourth generation. But just as there are generational curses, I'm equally convinced there are also generational blessings."

Some of our problems are cultural, some are social, some are economic. But God is greater than all the limitations you're struggling with, and that's a point Bishop makes very well in this lesson. "I don't care what your background is," Bishop says, "I can tell you something. The reason that God brought you here is so that the curses that have been running down through your family can be broken. Maybe your situation is not mine, but whatever is keeping you from receiving God's full blessing can be removed and broken right now. You can be the first of a new breed. You can be the first of your kind!

"That's why He is calling you right now out of your wasted past, so He can snatch you into the kingdom of God. He wants to break down generations of addiction to lust, poverty, depression, and disappointment. Whatever it is that's been running through your family, God can break it down right now. You truly can be the first of your kind. And if you accept what He has to offer, you can teach your children what they need to learn. I don't care if it's how to fish. Teach them, and show the next generation how to benefit from what you've learned.

"If you come to God, you will be in the Light. You will have the Power. Once you get an idea of what you're fighting, you can break it. That may mean that you have to make a new commitment to stay with that husband or wife you've been fighting. Maybe you feel frustrated and want to quit. Or maybe your background has been fighting you. But with Christ as your Power Source, you will have the strength to fight the frustration and confusion, and you can just break the spirit of defeat and get the power flowing once again in your life."

One of the first things I discovered as a professional athlete is that money is a major test of character. If you use it right, it can be a blessing; if you misuse it, however, it can destroy you. You may need a strategy for your finances. That may mean learning to discipline yourself and stop buying that junk that you know you can't afford and stop getting into debt and wondering why God ain't blessing you! God is blessing you, but you're living above your means. And you're going to have to get a program for the situation you're in and quit trying to look wonderful so you can be wonderful and let God bring you out of all your past mistakes.

You don't need a miracle. You need to be a better administrator over what you've got. You need to give God the keys to your life so He can give you the keys to the kingdom. And over a period of time, He's going to add to you and build you up. But you wouldn't invest in a company that's going bankrupt would you? God wouldn't either.

In concluding the session on how to gain a proper understanding of power, Bishop says that what God's looking at is your mind and how you think and what you do with what He gives you. Just like you do with your children, before God can give you what He has in store for you He has to be sure you're ready for it. He has to know you can handle it, and He can't trust you if you're out there glorifying yourself and living a lie. So God's with you. He loves you more than you'll ever know, but He's watching to see how you will respond.

chapter fourteen

USING YOUR TALENTS

If you want to be effective, you've got to find out what your gift is, and that process always begins with God. You go to God and say, "Father, why have You created me? What is distinctive about me? Before I go up against Goliath, show me the one thing I've got that if I work it, it will change my whole life. What is my slingshot?" The Bible says, "A man's gift makes room for him, and brings him before great men" (Prov. 18:16). So in the middle section of his teaching on power, money, and sex, Bishop Jakes says that if you want to be productive and effective in your life, you've got to know what your gift is before you can proceed on to the next step.

You say, "God, if You will show me my gift, I don't need You to give me money. I don't need no house, just give me some trees and I'll build my own house. I can build my own airplane, Lord, if You'll just show me how to mine the steel." Your gift will make room for you and take you before great men. So what is your gift? Do you know? Among the many gifts you've been given, generally there is one primary gift, and there are usually other gifts that will unlock different things. There's a gift that unlocks your marriage, and you need to know what it is!

When God was ready to use Moses in a special way, He put him on the back side of the desert. And one day God said, "Okay, Moses, let Me show you something. Stick your hand in your shirt." Moses stuck his hand in his shirt and when he pulled it out it came out white as snow. It was leprous. It was disfigured and defiled. But then God said, "Stick it in again," and Moses did and when he pulled it out this time it came out clean.

God said, "Okay, now throw down your rod." Moses did as he was told and his rod turned into a serpent. God said, "Pick it up." He did and it turned back into a rod. God said pour out some water; he did and it turned to blood. Do you see what God was doing? He was showing Moses his gift. He showed him his gift while he was still in the small stage, while he was on the back side of the desert. And once Moses learned how to operate his gift, God said, "Now I'm going to take you before great men."

Moses walked into the house of Pharaoh and told him, "God said let My people go, and if you don't do it, check this out!" He stuffed his hand in his shirt and threw down his rod, or whatever it was he actually did to show Pharaoh God's power and, trust me, Pharaoh got the point! You know the story. It took a visitation of plagues to shake him enough to loose all the captives, but Moses used God's gifts to set His people free. Listen. You'll know you're a man or woman of God when you can work your gifts like that.

Because a lot of people know me, Bishop has used me as an example from time to time. He says "Deion Sanders is who he is because he learned how to use his gift. And through that gift he has access to fame and fortune and public recognition, because of a gift. But we're all here because of our gifts, whatever they may be. We meet one another because of our gifts. But you can't even take credit for your gift, because ultimately it comes from God."

People say that Bishop T. D. Jakes is one of the best recognized and most quoted preachers in America today. But if that's true, how did it happen? Was it just some sort of spontaneous combustion? Of course not. The gift doesn't start when the camera comes on. It started back in the clay hills of West Virginia, in storefront churches, around potbellied stoves, in obscurity. Step by step, the ministry grew to the point that today when people say, "Where did this guy come from?" people answer, "He was on the back side of the desert practicing his stuff!"

But nobody can fight with their hands tied behind their backs. I've been broke and had really hard times and I understand that. But maybe all your needs are met and you're doing fine, so all this stuff about struggling just sounds alien to you. If that's the case, then let me ask you something: For all you make, do you really have enough to show for it? Do you honestly believe that you're all you were meant to be? And if not, why not?

Being Wise Stewards

In Matthew 25:14–29, Jesus tells a most remarkable parable. Look at what He says:

> For the kingdom of heaven is as a man travelling into a far country, who called his own servants, and delivered unto them his goods. And unto one he gave five talents, to another two, and to another one; to every man according to his several ability; and straightway took his journey.
>
> Then he that had received the five talents went and traded with the same, and made them other five talents. And likewise he that had received two, he also gained other two. But he that had received one went and digged in the earth, and hid his lord's money.
>
> After a long time the lord of those servants cometh, and reckoneth with them. And so he that had received five talents came and brought other five talents, saying, Lord, thou deliveredst unto me five talents: behold, I have gained beside them five talents more. His lord said unto him, Well done, thou good and faithful servant: thou hast been faithful over a few things, I will make thee ruler over many things: enter thou into the joy of thy lord.
>
> He also that had received two talents came and said, Lord, thou deliveredst unto me two talents: behold, I have gained two other talents beside them. His lord said unto him, Well done, good and faithful servant; thou hast been faithful over a few things, I will make thee ruler over many things: enter thou into the joy of thy lord.

Then he which had received the one talent came and said, Lord, I knew thee that thou art an hard man, reaping where thou hast not sown, and gathering where thou hast not strawed: And I was afraid, and went and hid thy talent in the earth: lo, there thou hast that is thine.

His lord answered and said unto him, Thou wicked and slothful servant, thou knewest that I reap where I sowed not, and gather where I have not strawed: Thou oughtest therefore to have put my money to the exchangers, and then at my coming I should have received mine own with usury. Take therefore the talent from him, and give it unto him which hath ten talents. For unto every one that hath shall be given, and he shall have abundance: but from him that hath not shall be taken away even that which he hath. (KJV)

Okay, check this out. The king was about to leave for a far country and he called his trusted servants together. First question: Are you God's servant? If you want to receive His gifts, you've got to be a servant. But notice that the passage also says that he "delivered unto them his goods." So really, your gift is not your gift after all—it's His gift. He's just flowing it through you.

If you've got any favor, if you've got any money, if you've got any power, it's not yours alone. Whatever it is, if you've got it, it may be a breakthrough for you, but it's from God. But here's another question: When you were born and you came into this world, how much money did you have? And when you die and that line goes straight across the machine, how much money are you taking with you? Well, that's how much you've got.

The Old Testament character Job knew all about that. He said, "Naked I came from my mother's womb, and naked shall I return there. The LORD gave, and the LORD has taken away; blessed be the name of the LORD" (Job 1:21). But here, the Bible says, the householder called unto him his servants and divided unto them his goods. A talent by today's standards would be around a thousand dollars, and it says he divided unto each "according to his abilities." He gave to one servant five talents, to another two, and to the third he gave one talent. But you say, "What? According to his ability? But I thought God was fair! If God is fair it seems like He ought to give everybody the same thing and the same amount."

No, He never said that, and it's a waste of time for you to be jealous of other people's gifts. God doesn't give everyone the same thing and He doesn't give everyone the same amount. He said the householder gave to each a different amount and then He tells you how he divided it—on the basis of the servant's demonstrated ability. God gives you what He knows you can handle.

Whether you do handle it or not, He wouldn't give it to you unless He knew that you have the capacity to handle it. If God gives you a gift, He has already assessed that it's within your power to work it. Because God never asks you to do anything that He won't enable you to do.

At this very moment God is watching you to see what you're going to do with what He has given you. He gave you life. He gave you gifts. He gave you resources, family, children, and now He's standing there watching you. He says, "Show Me what you can do with that." And you're wasting time complaining, "I ain't got enough help. I got to build a house and all I got is these dumb trees!" You have to devise a plan—through prayer and meditation and thought—to decide what you're going to do with what you've got.

Bishop Jakes also tells this story:

> One time I was ministering to a guy who was in the final stages of AIDS, and I said, "Man, what you gonna do with the life you got?" He was just sitting there in the house and his mother told me he wouldn't get out or do anything. He just sat in the back of the house in his room all day, moaning and complaining about his life. So I said, "You mean to tell me that you're getting ready to die and you're going to spend the last few days of your life just sitting in this room?!"
>
> I said, "Don't you want to go somewhere or see something? What you want to do?"
>
> He said, "Well, I want to feel the sun on my face."
>
> I said, "You ain't gonna feel the sun inside this house!"
>
> So I ask you now: What you gonna do with what you've got left? That's the issue. Do you believe in divine healing? Do you believe that God can heal you, change you, prepare you for something,

and make your life right again? Yes? Okay then, you had better seize the day!

Paul encouraged his young disciple Timothy when he was down, saying, "God has not given us a spirit of fear, but of power and of love and of a sound mind" (2 Tim. 1:7). If you let fear set upon you, it will rob you of the gift of life. It will take away your drive and your self-confidence. It can even damage your faith. Whatever it is you want in life today, you ought to go for it. If you woke up this morning and you weren't dead, you should have got up out of that bed going for it. Go for it! You ought to go if you have to come back!

Think of the apostle Peter when he stepped out of that old boat on the Sea of Galilee and walked on the water to meet Jesus. He only got about halfway before he started thinking about what he was doing out there, thinking about the law of gravity and the consistency of H_2O, and suddenly he started to sink. But you'll never hear me talk Peter down. Some preachers will say, "If Peter just had more faith he wouldn't have gotten into trouble." But I say, "Would you just look at Peter! He took a chance. He risked it. He put everything on the line." I mean, I want to be close to the answer instead of hanging out with the problem.

The Bible says Jesus stuck out His hand and pulled Peter up out of the water and began to walk him back to the boat. And I can just hear all those guys on the boat saying, "Oh, Peter, you got in trouble didn't you? We didn't get in trouble, but look at you. If it wasn't for the Lord you'd have lost everything. You almost lost your family, your business, and your life. You stepped out of the boat and got in trouble didn't you?"

And I hear Peter saying, "Yeah, but at least I got to go!"

Learning Your Lessons

Peter learned some things about God that he would never have known just hanging around the boat. There are some things that you will only learn about God when you step off and discover what God is saying to you. Are you hearing what I'm saying? God has given you abilities. Now He wants to see you use them. He's not asking you to have more IQ than He gave you. He's not asking you to keep up with what other people are doing. He says, "I'm just asking you for everything I gave you. I expect you to turn a profit."

Look at what He gave you and check the profit and loss. If I give you a million dollars, and you've got a million dollars worth of bills, you're just as poor as you can be. Because profit is what you have left when the transaction is over. And God demands that you turn a profit, not just get by on the month.

In the passage in Matthew 25, the wrath of the householder is reserved for the one servant who didn't risk anything. He did not take his gift and use it to turn a profit, he buried it, hid it, put it aside out of harm's way; but that was precisely what the master didn't want him to do. He said, "Risk it! Invest it. Use it, but don't let it just lie there and gather dust."

God gives you what He knows you can handle and He says to you, "Now risk it! Invest it. Use it!" He hasn't given you more than you can handle. When He handed out the manna in the wilderness, God gave according to need. To the smaller families, He gave a smaller amount; to the larger families, He gave more. That's why God hates jealousy, and He tells us not to measure ourselves by other people. Because God never promised to give every man the same amount or the same thing.

Bishop says that too often we have the notion that fairness means equality in all thing, but that's not really true. You don't have to worry about trying to be what people call fair. What people call fair is when you give everybody the same thing. But that's not wise. You've got to allocate blessings according to ability, performance, faithfulness, and function. To the more He gives more, to the less He gives less. If a guy don't produce nothing, he don't make nothing. That doesn't bother me. That just makes good sense.

Now if I'm ministering what I'm supposed to be ministering, certain things ought to be coming into your mind about your business, your finances, your marriage, your life. Faces ought to be coming to mind, and all the little things you've done. That's the Holy Spirit underlining what you're hearing and seeing here, and that's just for you.

But let me tell you about a passage of Scripture that radically changed my life.

> Blessed is the man that walketh not in the counsel of the ungodly,
> nor standeth in the way of sinners, nor sitteth in the seat of the

scornful. But his delight is in the law of the LORD; and in his law doth he meditate day and night. And he shall be like a tree planted by the rivers of water, that bringeth forth his fruit in his season; his leaf also shall not wither; and whatsoever he doeth shall prosper. (Ps. 1:1–3)

What Bishop Jakes discovered was that sometimes the word of God is revolutionary, that is, it turns your thinking around completely. In this most remarkable passage, God says, if you're going to be blessed, then you can't walk in the wisdom of this world. So you've got to get rid of all that dead wisdom in your life.

Some of that stuff comes from how you were raised. Some of it is prejudice, as it relates to races, genders, denominations, and many other things. I don't even mean the hateful, bad kinds of prejudice. I'm not talking about the 98-proof stuff or that cross-burning stuff. I'm not talking about the Nation of Islam either. I'm talking about that nice little neat little stuff. You know what I'm talking about.

It's the counsel of the ungodly that's still in your head. Some of it is how they taught you that you ought to treat the opposite sex. Young men who see their daddy smack their mama up against the refrigerator, and saying, "That's the way you got to treat 'em, son." That's the counsel of the ungodly. Going to work at places where you let what ungodly people say about Christians affect your attitude about your church and your faith.

Maybe what you hear out there won't affect you enough to make you leave the church or walk away from God, but sooner or later this little disgruntled spirit will begin to creep in and you won't even know where it's coming from. It's from the stuff you heard, and that's the counsel of the ungodly.

God says, if you want to be blessed you cannot walk in the counsel of the ungodly. That means you will allow nobody to counsel you who's worse off than you. And the next phrase says, "Nor standeth in the way of sinners." Don't let anything about you hinder other people from coming to Jesus. "Nor sitteth in the seat of the scornful." What does that mean? It says, even if you don't understand what's going on, shut up! Don't ever let it be said that you kicked against what God was doing.

If you want to be blessed, get with the program, flow with the ministry, catch the vision, and be a part of the solution and not part of the problem.

If you want to be blessed. then don't sit in the seat of the scornful. If you're not going to flow with it, then get out of it. But don't sit there, murmuring and complaining, because that's the seat of the scornful, and you're going to bring a curse on yourself if you keep that up.

But then the psalmist says, "His delight is in the law of the LORD; and in his law doth he meditate day and night. And he shall be like a tree planted by the rivers of water, that bringeth forth his fruit in his season; his leaf also shall not wither; and whatsoever he doeth shall prosper." I want to be like a tree planted by streams of living water. I want to be a stable man. I want my church, my wife, my kids, and especially my God to be able to count on me. I want to be a dependable man. I want to be like a tree planted by a river of living water, that is stable in good times and bad times.

When we seek to live that way we discover what it means to have the abundant life that Jesus talked about when He said, "I have come that they may have life, and that they may have it more abundantly" (John 10:10). The abundant life means your life is rich. You might be having spring when everybody else is having winter. I can't get jealous of your spring because I know that when my winter is over, springtime is coming.

Anybody who is committed to God in this way will flourish. He will be a man "that bringeth forth his fruit in his season" and, He says, "his leaf also shall not wither." Your season will not come and go, but you will flourish in God's abundance. And then we have the last line. This is the line that changed my life. It says, "And whatsoever he doeth shall prosper."

That got in my head one day and it blew my mind. I had been trained to ask God to do something. "God, You do it! You do it, Lord!" And I was sitting back waiting on God to do it. I paid my tithes, Lord. Now I'm waiting on You to do it. I sowed my seed and gave my offering. Now I'm waiting on You to do it. I read the Scripture of healing and now I'm waiting on You to do it." And I didn't know that God was sitting there saying, "I've already released the blessing. And now I'm waiting on you to do it!"

When I understood that passage, it was like flashbulbs going off in my head. God was saying, "I'm waiting on you. I've given you the land, now I'm waiting on you to possess it. I've written out My deed of trust. It's already yours. Now drive out those little problems and possess the land. It's yours, but you've got to take authority over it in the name of Jesus. So why are you sitting there waiting on Me?! I'm waiting on you!" It says, "Whatsoever he doeth shall prosper."

Power, money, sex. What Bishop's teachings have taught me is not just that people have a problem with them, but that only divine guidance can give us the wisdom to use them correctly. They're such powerful forces, such powerful desires, such powerful stimulants to people today. In themselves, they're harmless. But if any of them gets out of balance, they can eat you alive. And that's why you need to let God refocus your heart and your desires, so that you can use these things as they were meant to be used. Paul says we are to flee from our unrighteous impulses so that we can "pursue righteousness, godliness, faith, love, patience, gentleness." We are to "fight the good fight of faith" so that we may one day "lay hold on eternal life" (1 Tim. 6:10–13).

Eternal life! Think of that! A better and richer life, not just for now but for all eternity. How much more encouragement do you need?

chapter fifteen

A BALANCED LIFE

I f you look at the covers of any of the major magazines written for men and women these days, you'll see articles about power, money, and sex. I don't care if it's a publication for working women or a men's bodybuilding magazine. It will say, "Ten Ways to Improve Your Sex Life." Every issue. "Seven Ways to Perform Better!" Why? Because they know people will buy that stuff.

No matter how virile or how spiritual you may seem to other people, in the back of everyone's mind, to some degree, there is an innate interest in power, money, and sex. One of the challenges for people who have come out of the world into the church is that they become a Christian and suddenly everything that was "normal" yesterday becomes taboo today.

They may be considered moral, upright, upstanding people in the community, but they've got somebody on the side. That's accepted in today's society. But then they get saved and all of a sudden it's like having a car wreck. Bam! They may come into the church and sing and praise the Lord on Sunday, but the minute somebody starts telling them to modify their sexual behavior, even if they want to do it, it becomes a struggle.

Bishop doesn't beat around the bush, and I like that about him. But especially when dealing with sexual problems, he goes right to the heart of the matter. "Here's the problem: No matter how righteous your heart may be, and no matter how much you are committed to serving God, your body is not saved. I may be the first person to tell you this, and it may shock you, but just in case you haven't noticed it, your body isn't saved! It has not been changed."

Can't you see the hypocrisy in our attitudes abou these things? Bishop's example is right to the point. He says, "When I was a young person growing up in church, people would get saved and come down to the altar and accept Christ, and we would sing, "I looked at my hands and my hands looked new; I looked at my feet and they did, too! I started walking and I had a new walk; I started talking and I had a new talk!" Sounds wonderful. Big lie! Huge lie!

"The fact is, if you had a bunion on your foot before you got saved, as soon as you get home from church take your shoe off and see! That same old bunion is still right there! Your body has not received notification that you are saved, and when it does get the news it doesn't like it. Paul even says, 'I beat my body and make it my slave so that after I have preached to others, I myself will not be disqualified for the prize' (1 Cor. 9:27 NIV).

"He knew it: Your body is not saved. You've been saved in your spirit and you're being changed in your mind, but your physical nature is yet to be changed. If it was changed you wouldn't be tempted in that area, because it wouldn't be there anymore."

The Way of All Flesh

Sexuality is an area of struggle for a lot of people today, and if you are in Christ you must take this under subjection to your will, and let Christ show you how to control your body and to control those lustful emotions. That's the only way. The Bible calls it "sins of the flesh," and they're there at every stage of your life, just waiting to get the upper hand.

Think about this: Bishop says that if a young man is promiscuous in his youth, he will more than likely ruin the life of some woman in his life. But if he's promiscuous when he's older, it's more likely some woman will ruin him. So at every age you have to gain control over that aspect of your character and your human nature.

You may say, "Well, it's not a struggle for me today." But I must tell you, sooner or later it will be, and you can't wait until then to solve the problem. You've got to prepare now so that you will have the resources to resist temptation when the time does come.

Bishop speaks with people from all walks of life, with all sorts of problems, and he says, "I sometimes counsel men who are struggling in this area, and some of them who have come from a promiscuous background will tell me they're trying to get out of their wives the things they feel they need. And they cannot figure out how to do it. But the first thing they need to understand is that men and women are very different in this area. Men are stimulated by what they see while women are stimulated by how they feel. Sex for a woman doesn't start in bed, it starts in the living room.

"Most men are too quick on the draw. She has worked all day and she comes home and she's got tricycles and homework and chicken dinner to make. So she's supposed to go from being a workhorse to a mommy to a nursemaid to a sex goddess in the course of two hours' time? That's quite a metamorphosis to make.

"But one thing that makes it easier for her is if she's reminded that beneath all these other tasks is a man who cares, who cares deeply, and who stimulates her mind and her emotions. He appreciates and affirms who she is and he shows genuine affection in little ways. He calls her now and then just to say, 'Hi, honey. I was just thinking about you, and I just wanted you to know that I love you.' That's what she needs to hear."

Now, here's something Bishop talks about that you may need to read more than once. "The Bible says, 'Marriage is honourable in all, and the bed undefiled: but whoremongers and adulterers God will judge' (Heb. 13:4 KJV). You see, marriage is a covenant between a man and a woman established and sanctioned by God. It is honorable. It is holy. But whoremongers and adulterers are under the judgment of God. I call them Sneaky Petes, church playboys, sex bandits. God says to them, "I will judge you!" And no generation in history has been more judged for promiscuity than our own.

"Even people who do not know Christ are starting to adopt our morality. They're beginning to realize that sex can be deadly. But I challenge those who are in the faith: Don't let them fool around and be wiser in their way than you are in yours. You've got Christ but you're still living like the devil. They've got the devil and they're starting to live like Christians. Ain't that a mess!? God says, 'If you play, you're going to pay.'"

As the leader of a church of more than 15,000 members, Bishop Jakes sees people at all stages of faith, and he says that "There are too many men in all walks of life today who are struggling with these issues, and too many of them are in the church. I shouldn't say 'struggling,' I should say 'in it.' They're in the pews on Sunday morning singing all the hymns, and two hours later they're off reveling in adultery, pornography, homosexuality, or having multiple affairs. 'Praise the Lord, I'm Deacon Sneaky Pete!' But God says, 'I will judge you!'"

Bishop Jakes says he sees in his spirit a time when people won't have to lie, when men and women can be honest and say, "Hey, I've had a real experience with Christ and I know He has touched my life, but I have a real problem in this area. I'm struggling with crack, or with homosexuality, or an affair, or with pornography." And unless we face our challenges in that way and dump all that stuff at the foot of the cross, then we are living a lie. Any time you stop being honest, you can't be healed. You're holding those dark secrets thinking you can just live a lie, but you already know that sores that are covered don't heal.

What we've got to do is get rid of what we have experienced so we can run into what God created. Can you believe that what He created may be better than what you have experienced? It is the struggle of transformation to forget those things which are behind and to reach to those things which are before.

Paul says, "I press toward the mark for the prize of the high calling of God in Christ Jesus" (Phil. 3:14 KJV). Do you hear that? That's the language of the runner straining toward the tape, veins popping, breath searing through his nostrils, every sinew and every muscle concentrated on that one thing: the mark, the goal, the prize that is just beyond his outstretched fingers.

That's the whole issue, to let go of those things which are behind so that you can grab hold of that which is just ahead. In sexual experience, your early experiences, right or wrong, tend to dictate your tastes and interests. A certain look, a certain smell, a certain touch. And you are a combination of everywhere you've been, everything you've touched, and everything that has touched you.

Our memories and experiences, Bishop says, are like movies that we rewind and replay in our heads for the rest of our lives. But the problem is, sometimes everything that touched you wasn't right. And you may be doing everything in your power to live a new life and walk with Christ and all of a sudden, boom, here come the old movies from your past, right up on the television screen of your mind. And you think, *I remember things I can't even talk about.* And if you linger in that, the devil has you right where he wants you.

If you don't break the old habits, he'll start pulling you right back down where you used to be. If he can't get in the front way, he'll come in the back way. And the dangerous thing about it is that he knows where all your doors are. He knows where your windows are. He has cased the house and he knows that the doors and windows to your sexuality and your vulnerability to sin are right around your past experiences.

The Door to Your Heart

Your brokenness, your wounds, incidents, accidents, adversities, molestations, whatever it was you experienced. Those memories, that's the door he's going to come through. Now some of you are really uncomfortable. You don't want to hear this. But I'm here to tell you, the enemy is accessing you through that door right now. Something you've been through lets him know what buttons to push. Because if you'll notice, the devil don't waste time offering you stuff you don't want. He knows where to knock!

The Bible says, "We are not ignorant of his devices" (2 Cor. 2:11). We need to understand that as a man or woman of God we're going to have to do spiritual warfare, and it's going to be a long war, because periodically the devil's going to come back. The Bible says that when the devil tempted Jesus in the wilderness, he left Him for a season. So seasonally that devil is going to come back.

You can lay out on the floor and roll your eyes up into your head and turn into a watermelon, but when you come out of it he's going to be there knocking at the door, whispering, "You home? Hello! It's me, let me in." And if you pause even one second, he'll be whispering, "You don't have to tell nobody. They wouldn't understand."

And there you are sitting up in church, singing hymns and praising the Lord, and just listening to him knocking, and you can't even tell anybody what's going through your mind. That's the warfare I'm talking about. That's the battle you're in. And it's a battle we all fight every day, because the devil knows our weaknesses and he never gives up.

When dealing with the issue of sin, Bishop goes to the Scriptures, and he points out that Proverbs 14:34 says, "Righteousness exalts a nation, but sin is a reproach to any people." All the things you've been planning, all the good intentions you've been storing up, and all the plans you've made to serve God won't mean a thing if you don't shut that door and padlock it. You have to get to the point where, like clockwork, whenever he comes around, you can say, "I hear you knockin', but you can't come in!"

Bishop Jakes says that one of the things that led to his writing the books *Woman, Thou Art Loosed!* and *Loose That Man and Let Him Go* was counseling so many people who were struggling. Many people—including many who didn't even look like they ever had a problem in this area—were deeply troubled about sexual problems. But one day, maybe years down the road, something happened and they would have a fight and suddenly one of them would break the code of silence and you see what was really underneath the surface.

Do you know what makes divorce so terrible? It's that when you divorce from somebody, they carry your secrets out of your house. Psychologists will tell you that you recover better when a spouse dies than you do from a divorce, because they know all your secrets and all your business and now all your business is in the bed with somebody else. And you can never be sure what they're talking about tonight.

One of the things that will always stop you from winning over sin is by focusing on it. You spend all your time concentrating on that one thing that you need to forget until it just drives you crazy. Let me tell you something: The best way to get loose from sin is to get distracted by righteousness. Until all of a sudden you're so caught up with what God is calling you to that you get the grace to leave what He's calling you from. God never called a man from anything without calling him to something better.

At this point, Bishop Jakes has tried to remove all the props from under our excuses and our delusions about sin. When we finally see what's true and right, we have recognized that God will not tolerate those excuses. Jesus said, "You shall know the truth, and the truth shall make you free" (John 8:32). You'll never be free as long as you're lying. You'll be free when you step into His presence and say, "This is who I really am and I need You to heal me and change me." Instead of trying to change everybody to fit your perversion and changing your spouse and your circumstances, you need to quit trying to change everybody and come to the altar and say, "Lord, change me."

Maybe you've never been honest about your sexuality. But maybe it's time for you to deal with those things and break the code of silence. Jim Bakker said something very interesting. When he talked about all his experiences with all the stuff that made the headlines for such a long period of time, he said it all came back to a secret he had carried around all his life—that he had never been touched correctly as a child. And out of his abuse came obsessive behavior. And he had to go all the way to hell and back before he could talk about it.

Maybe you need to face up to your own situation so that you can break the bondage to sin that has gripped you for so long. Or maybe you need to take a more serious look at who you are as a child of God so you can use the equipment as God intended it to be used instead of wasting it on those trivial attachments and cheap illusions that will destroy you.

Wherever you are, you need to get transparent with God. Talk to Him about your rage, abuse, frustrations, perversions, or anything else that's eating you up inside and keeping you from being the man or woman of God that He designed you to be. Can you open up and talk to Him honestly about being out of balance and out of control?

When you're a professional athlete, you get around. You get the chance to see and do things other people can only imagine. Sometimes that can be very good, but it can also be dangerous if you're not seeing your life from a long-range point-of-view. As he reaches the end of his teaching on power, money, and sex, Bishop Jakes asks some pointed questions. He says: Can you face your own lust, your personal problems, your constant battle with emotional pain? You've got things in your life you need to do and be, but that enemy keeps knocking at your door. Now is the time to deal with that stuff. Don't put it off. You can never be all that God planned for you to be when your life is out of balance.

In itself, sex is not evil. God designed and ordained sexuality and gave it to us as a symbol of the unity and the fulfillment that He Himself desires to have with His church. In itself, power is not evil. The Bible says, "But ye shall receive power, after that the Holy Ghost is come upon you: and ye shall be witnesses unto me" (Acts 1:8 KJV). God wants you to use the power He gives you for good.

The Bible also says that "the love of money is a root of all kinds of evil, for which some have strayed from the faith in their greediness, and pierced themselves through with many sorrows" (1 Tim. 6:10). The love of money may be the root of evil, but money in itself is not evil unless it is abused and misused. If it is allowed to control your thoughts and actions, money can destroy you and pierce your heart with sorrows. But when your life is balanced and you've given God the keys to your heart, it can be a tremendous blessing.

Finally, Proverbs 18:16 says, "A man's gift makes room for him, and brings him before great men." That means your gift can take you before great men, and whatever God has designed you to be can bear real fruit and bring you great joy. God has already given you a gift, and that gift will make a place for you. But you have to understand who you are in the kingdom of God, and that means you have to be connected to the Power Supply. Are you? Do you have that kind of power? Do you want to have?

Here's the way. Jesus says, "I am the way, the truth, and the life. No one comes to the Father except through Me" (John 14:6). In another place He says, "I am the resurrection and the life. He who believes in Me, though he may die, he shall live. And whoever lives and believes in Me shall never die" (John 11:25–26). Now that's power! It's the greatest power of all, and it is available for you right now. All you have to do is confess your need, admit your failure and your sin, and ask Jesus to come into your life.

Can you do that? Will you do it? You may have the best battery in town, but until you get connected to Him, you're not going anywhere. If you want to tap into God's power supply, then this is where you put the plug. Jesus is the way—not a way, but THE way. Why not trust Him today?

chapter sixteen

TELLING IT STRAIGHT

The title of this book, *Power, Money, and Sex*, is somewhat provocative, and I chose it because those are things that most people think about and deal with every day. I have seen how power, money, and sex change people's lives. And I've seen that most of the time it's not the kind of change that makes you happy. It's almost never the kind of change that helps you grow in faith. Instead, it's the kind of change that comes through abuse, and it ends up hurting you and everybody around you.

I know guys who have misused those things while they were playing the game. They were into everything you could imagine and living as if there was no tomorrow, and then suddenly tomorrow came. They lived and played as if they were invincible, then they had a serious injury on the field and everything in their life changed. When that happens, it's not just a sports injury; it's a fatality. Because in a lot of cases it's the end of the road for their careers, and suddenly the dream is over.

Now if the guy has prepared for that, and if he has some understanding of the risks and the potential consequences of the game, he can probably survive a career-ending injury. Maybe he will do just fine. He can go on to other things and he will always have those great memories of his days in the pros. But I can tell you that there aren't a lot of guys thinking that way early in their careers.

I've seen it so many times, particularly when they've come to me for money or for advice after things start to fall apart. Anybody seeing how they lived, how they acted, and how they performed on the field would have assumed that they had it all together. But that's not necessarily the case. It doesn't even have to be an injury. Sometimes it's just changes in the person, changes inside their head, changes in their lifestyle or the people they're associating with.

A divorce can do it, and sometimes a casual word or something in the media can do it. One week they may be the hottest player in baseball, or the Most Valuable Player for the entire NFL, and the very next week they couldn't make a play if their life depended on it. Suddenly scoring a touchdown or getting a base hit is totally out of the question.

They say fame is fickle. Football is fickle, too. And baseball is fickle. Anything you depend on for your meaning in life that takes you away from the real meaning in life—which is your one-on-one relationship with Jesus Christ—is fickle. Anything else that you give first place in your life will let you down if you focus on the wrong things.

I know a lot of entertainers—including singers, rappers, actors, whatever—and the common denominator they all have is their fame. It's not fortune. Most of them don't even have a fortune. But they all have fame. If they get money, they spend it. If they get houses and cars and jewelry and possessions, they use them up and destroy them. If they have relationships, they trash those, too. And they end up with nothing. No fame, no fortune, no future. And at twenty-five or thirty years old, they end up feeling their lives are over.

I've been very close to M. C. Hammer for many years, and I've seen what he's been through. I love him. Hammer is a great and dear friend to this day. He was the original. There was nobody doing what he does when Hammer first hit it big. He put rap on the charts and changed the entire direction of urban music for several years. He made it big and he lived high. But one day the music seemed to just stop, and his fame and fortune were just chewed up by other things.

I've always said that Hammer's problem was that he loved too much. He loved the life that he was living, and he loved people. He employed all his friends, and he had this tremendous payroll. I used to go to his house in San Francisco and I'd see all these people around him, most of them doing nothing, and I'd say, "Hammer, what does that guy do? Or what about that guy over there, what does he do?"

He didn't know. They didn't do anything, they were just living off his success. I remember him saying, "Deion, I wish I had the courage to say no."

In those days, Hammer was just a guy who lived for the moment. He never thought that one day it would all be over. No one could ever have guessed that Hammer's time would come. He was just as intelligent then as he is now. He was just as caring then as he is now. He was just as capable then as he is now. But there was no accountability, and fame and fortune nearly destroyed him.

Ultimately his success wrecked his family, and it took years to mend those relationships. He was a Christian, a believer, and he knew the truth. But success is seductive and he was seduced into a lifestyle that he knew was wrong. But when I see him today, I see a totally new man. Hammer paid the price of that lifestyle, and now Christ is rebuilding him into a man after His own heart.

The return of M. C. Hammer will really be something to see. I'm excited that he has a new career in gospel music, using his talents for God's glory this time instead of his own. So hang on! You'll be seeing big things from Hammer very soon. But how tragic to have to learn those important lessons the hard way.

Turning the Corner

Power is a hard thing for some people to get a handle on. When they think about power, they think about politicians or public officials. But that's not all it is. You can have personal power with your family, your friends, your teammates, your community, and even larger groups. Some people have the capacity to influence the whole world, and that can be either good or bad, depending on how they use it and what their motivation is. Adolf Hitler turned the world upside down for a decade or two, and the whole world got a look at his kind of power, which was a terrible evil.

Jesus Christ has turned the world upside down for nearly two thousand years, based purely on His ministry of love and His message about how we can enjoy a personal relationship with Him. That kind of power is for our good. But in between those two extremes, there are a million examples of men and women who have used their personal power to influence others. What's important to realize is that everybody has the ability to influence other people. The question is, will they use it for evil or for good?

I was in the store recently buying some fishing equipment and some people came up to me and said, "Deion, we just praise the Lord for your testimony!" I didn't know anybody knew I was there. I wasn't thinking about my influence or who might be there while I was shopping. But these folks just came up and said thank you because they saw that I was having an influence because of my faith. You may never know who you've influenced in this world, but people are watching, and one way or another someone is being influenced by you.

I was always accepted in the 'hood growing up. My people respected me, so that gave me a certain amount of power and influence. They knew I was real and that I was trying to be reliable. They expected certain things from me, but they trusted me and knew I would never lie to them. But sometimes people who have a certain level of trust will misuse it and mislead people. It happens all the time. If you choose to be decent and honest, people will want to follow you. But if you just want to go somewhere and be ignorant, there are people who'll go along and be ignorant, too. But you have to choose.

We're seeing more good examples in the sports world today than we have in a long time, but I have some concerns about that. As I said earlier, I worry about this whole idea of "role models." I don't agree with that. That's a kind of power, but I don't think parents should entrust their responsibilities to influence and raise decent kids to athletes or anyone else. A role model is just a model playing a role. It's not the role itself, it's a game of make-believe, and that's never as good as the real thing.

Next to Jesus Christ, the best role model and standard bearer your child will ever have is you. Just because I'm on television for two or three hours on Sunday doesn't mean I have the right or the responsibility to teach your kids how to act. It's not the NFL or Major League Baseball that they need to focus on. What will mean the most to them is the other stuff that happens on Sunday, with you, your family, your church, and the community where you live.

I worry about families that expect me or any other athlete to be a "role model." I'm not going to be there to take your kid to school, to pick him up, to help him with his homework, or to buy his clothes. That's your responsibility, and he'll learn a lot more about the meaning of life by seeing a godly example from you than by watching me make an interception or tackle somebody on the football field.

Dangerous Illusions

I didn't know very much about power, money, and sex when I was coming up, but I was always on that train called "The Little Engine That Could." One day I realized that if I was ever going to be anybody I needed to get on that train, and I've never gotten off. A lot of people have doubted me over the years. Even coaches and athletic directors doubted me at times, but I never doubted myself. When I speak to young people in the schools, one of the things I always tell them is that they've got to believe in themselves. Because if they don't believe in themselves, nobody else will either.

There are lots of kids these days in all cultures and communities whose parents, families, and neighbors are just filling them up with a lot of negative junk, saying stuff like, "You're just no good and you'll never amount to anything." What do you think that kind of talk does to a young person's mind? When they hear stuff like that they're just devastated. But what they need to do is just turn it around. So I tell them not to be looking at anybody else or trying to act like somebody they're not, but to just be themselves and to believe in themselves.

Unfortunately, some kids are going to believe the negative programming and fall by the wayside. But I know that there will be others who will say, "I'm going to prove you wrong!" and they'll just see that negative feedback as a shove in the back, pushing them to do better, go faster, and think a little bigger than anybody else. That's how I was.

When people would put me down, I'd say, "Man, I'm going to prove you wrong!" My mother and my family didn't put me down, but there were other people who would be more than happy to do it. I remember a couple of coaches who seemed to take a perverse pleasure in putting down their players. But that just made me want to work harder, and I was always able to prove them wrong.

You know, kids listen to that stuff. But I'm honest with them, and they can see that I'm being real. I tell them the truth and I don't try to snow them with who I am or what I've accomplished in sports. I tell the girls, don't just focus on being pretty and sexy. Put something in your mind while you're in school. You'll find that most men want a woman they can talk to, somebody who knows things and who is intelligent and stimulating company and not just a pretty face. If nothing else, someday you may meet some guy who needs you to help him with his homework. So don't just focus on the physical stuff!

But I also say, you know, you're building a record in your life. Think of it like a police car following you. Sooner or later they're gonna run your plates and check to see what kind of record you've got. When they pull you over, they gonna talk to you about outstanding tickets and problems in your record. It's the same with a guy who's beginning to take an interest in you. He may talk to you and he may follow you around for a while, but if he starts to really get interested, he's gonna run your plates before he pulls you over.

He'll ask about you around the school. He'll check you out with your friends. Does she have a track record? Where has she been? If she's been with a lot of other guys, that's not the kind of girl he wants for a wife. He wants somebody special, clean, nice, who'll be a good friend, and maybe someday a wife and mother. So don't start building a rap sheet now while you're young, because if you do you're just fixing things so that no decent guy will ever take an interest in you. And when you do get pulled over, make sure your record is clear and clean.

That's why I say I'm honest and real with these young people. There are a lot of men who will tell a girl anything she wants to hear if he thinks he can score with her, and unless she has a better sense of values than that, she can let herself be destroyed. And it's not just for a day or a week, but for the rest of her life. Kids respond when I talk to them about these things because, first of all, they know I've been there. But, second, they know I love them and I really do care for them. I really do.

If you see how I play baseball or football, you know that there's still a lot of kid in me. I act like a kid, I like to horse around and have fun. But I also want to enjoy my life and never let my career get so serious that it's just another boring job. Sure, it's a job, but it's also a game! It's meant to be fun. It's meant to make people happy and excited, and so I've learned to make my job fun, and then to be open and honest about the things that really matter, both on and off the field.

The Next Generation

There are a lot of people who say the next generation coming up is already hopeless. But I'm not buying any of that. I believe these kids are the future, just like the song says. And no child is ever hopeless. God blessed all of us in some sort of way. The challenge is to figure out what your blessing is. What is your talent or gift? We all have them, so what's yours? This is so important, and that's one reason why I wanted to include the material from Bishop Jakes on that subject.

Not everybody could or should be an athlete. I say that every team has to have attorneys and doctors and coaches and public relations people and managers to help the team accomplish its goals. And it's the same with everyday life. Every young person needs to look deep down inside themselves and find out:

What is that one thing that represents who you really are? What is your talent, your interest, your gift, or your ambition? When you find that, your life will have a new sense of purpose and meaning, and then you can begin to educate those talents and instincts so you can become the best you can be in your chosen field.

Pastor David Forbes from Columbus Christian Center has been an important influence in my life. One of the first things I noticed about him was that this is a man who really loves people. He is an energetic, fun guy. When you're with David Forbes, you feel energized and excited about life.

He makes a joyful noise. His spirit is so pleasant and sweet. I've never seen him angry or upset. I've never seen him disturbed. But do you know why that is? Because God is a very real and constant presence in his life. Every day he walks with God and that has transformed him into a beautiful person.

Pastor Forbes is the same every day, and he has such a pleasant personality. He's somebody who is secure in who he is and in doing what God has called him to do. He's not interested in anything that I or anybody else can give him, but he's passionate about what God can give him.

God has truly blessed me in sending people like Pastor David Forbes and Bishop T. D. Jakes into my life—people who can get with me and hold me accountable and lead me in my spiritual walk.

Since Bishop Jakes lives in Dallas, where I live now, he's always nearby during the football season, and he provides the kind of spiritual nourishment my heart desires. When I'm up in Cincinnati playing baseball, Pastor David Forbes is nearby and he has become a friend, a brother, and a spiritual mentor to me. In addition, David is young enough that I can really relate to him one-on-one. He's energetic and fun-loving enough that he can really get through to me.

Bishop and David are different personalities. They have different gifts. They teach and interact with people in their own unique ways, but both are blessed by God, and both are filled with the love of Jesus. They may have different personalities and different approaches, but they both have the love of God and they're both honest and sincere men who have taught me a lot. They love their wives, their families, their churches and ministries, and they love God most of all.

These men aren't sissies. They're not some kind of wimpy, mealy-mouthed, limp-wristed Christians. They're powerful men. Men of God, like Joshua and Caleb—men who are "relevant"—meaning, they're making a difference in people's lives. As I think ahead to the prospect of my own career in the ministry, these two men have become my teachers and advisers. They're like my college and my graduate school rolled into one, demonstrating through their own lives how to minister the Word.

I believe that one way you can know the nature of your calling is by seeing who God puts you under. You can tell where God is taking you by the kind of people, and especially the kind of mentors, He puts into your life. And I can assure you, I know what a blessing it is to be learning under men of this stature. They are a blessing to me, and as mentors they are just unbelievable.

When you're living in the world and doing things your own way, you're around people who want something from you. The more successful you become, the more hangers-on you have. It's like, "What can you do for me today?" But these men aren't like that. They want to pour out what they have into me and into others who are eager to learn. But when they finish pouring it into you, they slap you on the behind and say, "Giddyup! Now go get 'em!"

You don't grow up in the faith overnight. In these last few chapters we've shared a lot about power, money, and sex, along with a lot of important insights into what it means to live the Christian life. But spiritual growth doesn't happen suddenly; it's more like a tree. You grow gradually, patiently, and you put down roots. Like an oak tree, faith needs time to grow. You need time alone with God. Growth involves what we do and what we don't do. It involves all our attitudes and feelings about our relationship with God.

Why do some people stop growing? Some people catch on fire and then one day they see that the embers have died down and they've grown cold. Why does that happen? Can you remember a time when you were on fire for the Lord? What happened to the fire? Are you still on fire? If not, who put your fire out? Who poured water on the flames of your love for God? You know, if you're not walking with Him each day, that's what will happen. The flames will just die down little by little if they're not being fanned.

Sometimes life can do a number on your passion and stomp out the embers of your passion for God. Oh, you may say you're serving Him, and you may show up at church on Sundays and go through all the motions now and then. But you know it's not the same thing anymore. But why is that? What happened to your first love?

We all go through changes, and that's natural. Growth involves change and if you're not changing in some way, then maybe you're not growing anymore. The strongest trees are those that have been exposed to winds and storms and stresses of various kinds. Did you ever notice that? Winds and storms don't destroy a tree that has deep roots. That only causes them to grow stronger. When the winds come, the tree sends its roots deeper and deeper. Is that what you're doing? Are you growing deep roots? Are you changing for the better? Or have you given up and started to sag and wilt and fade around the edges?

A tree grows best when it's exposed regularly to the light of the sun, and that's true for you and me, too. The Bible says that "God is light and in Him is no darkness at all" (1 John 1:5). Are you walking in the Light? Are you being exposed daily to the Son? Jesus says, "I am the way, the truth, and the life. No one comes to the Father except through Me" (John 14:6).

If you want to be in the light, then you need to be in the light of the Son of God. A tree that is strong grows toward the light. Christians who want to grow stronger and serve God will want to grow in the Light of God's love, through His Son, Jesus Christ.

The Bible says, "Train up a child in the way he should go, and when he is old he will not depart from it" (Prov. 22:6). That means you, mom and dad. Athletes have the ability to influence children and they know it. That's one reason the NFL is active with organizations like the United Way, the United Negro College Fund, and other charities. They want to channel all that influence into worthy causes.

But too often parents and kids aren't looking at the good things we do in the sports community as much as they're looking at the clothes, the cars, the jewelry, or the money we make as professional entertainers. If that's all they see, then they're looking at the wrong stuff. They don't know how we live. They don't know what problems we may have. They don't realize that some of us are being eaten alive by our problems, and some are on the verge of suicide.

The Power of Love

I used to think that power, money, and sex were everything. I didn't realize there was anything bigger than that, but now I know there is. Now I have a much better idea about the meaning of Jesus' words in Luke 12:48, where He says, "For unto whomsoever much is given, of him shall be much required: and to whom men have committed much, of him they will ask the more" (KJV).

If parents took their own roles more seriously they wouldn't need "role models" for their kids. If parents took the time to listen to their kids, to let them talk about their worries and their hopes, to ask them about their problems and their fears, then the kids wouldn't be running off and getting into trouble.

The reason so many girls are getting pregnant out of wedlock is because some boy gets close to them and whispers, "I love you." They don't mean it, of course. That boy doesn't love her in the least. As soon as he gets what he wants, he'll be out of there. But she is not hearing those words from her mama and daddy at home, so she gravitates to anybody who will say them to her, even if it's a lie.

"I love you." Those are the magic words that can steal a young person's heart. You know what they're going through. You know that this culture is putting a lot of junk in their heads. You know they've been taught that sex is cool and that it's okay to do anything they can get away with. It's all a lie, of course, and it will ruin their lives. But they don't hear that. I can tell you, it's Satan's biggest lie, and it's killing kids every day. But they are so desperate to hear somebody say the magic words, and really mean it, that they will risk everything for the sake of that lie.

Some of our young kids are being raised so fast and getting such a hard dose of reality at home, they feel as if they've become the parents and their parents are the kids. That's one of the reasons I grew up so quick, because I had to become the father in my household at one point. My biological father wasn't there. He wasn't reliable. So I wanted to do fatherly things. My stepfather was there but he wasn't really engaged with us. He just worked, smiled, and never complained, and he drank himself to sleep every night. But I felt like somebody had to be the daddy, so I became the daddy in my home.

There are a lot of kids, however, who don't respond that way. They've got too much pressure, too many disappointments, too many hurts, and they rebel and go the other way. I know that's happening. Maybe they don't have a strong mother; maybe they don't have a good sense of self-respect; maybe they don't have a skill or a talent that can help them break out of it, so they lash out instead.

Some of these kids will get into gangs and start trying stuff that will only hurt them in the end. But there is a way out of that trap. Somebody has to get straight with them and tell them that all those things are deadly, and if they keep it up they're going to get burned. But most of all, somebody needs to tell them they're loved, and let them know that God has a wonderful plan for their lives.

If you can just convince them of that, then nothing can stop them from becoming the best man or woman they can be. And that's where the power really begins.

chapter seventeen

PRIME TIME

U ntil recently, I had only been to two funerals in my life, and both of them were my fathers—my biological father and my stepfather. Later I went to the funeral of a woman who was my athletic director in high school. She was a dear woman, and I had a chance to say a few words at her funeral. But for most of my life I've been protected from very much contact with death and dying.

Going to the funerals of my fathers was very hard for me. The Lord prepared me each step of the way. But my fathers were so special because they were really more like my children than my fathers. Most of the time when I was growing up, our roles were reversed. I would always be telling them, "Don't smoke, don't drink, just get your butt home. You need to start doing right." That taught me a lot, but it also created an unusual bond between us.

Everything changed when I went to college, but up to that time I had been the man of the house. My stepfather was calm, compassionate, laidback, very hard working, very determined, but basically he was reserved and not really engaged with us as a family. My biological father, on the other hand, was the exact opposite. He represented the whole opposite side. He was outgoing, flashy, flamboyant, outspoken.

Daddy Buck was my homey, my partner. He was a player. Life, love, women, he had it all scoped. He was charismatic, charming, debonair. He was the flashy one, and always a dresser. He was the real Prime Time!

I remember riding around with him in a limousine, and he'd be saying, "Now look here, baby boy, you better move those snakeskins from beside my gators. My gators gonna eat you up, Podnah!" I got a kick out of that. He had some bad habits and most of the time I couldn't do anything with him, so at one point I asked my friend M. C. Hammer if he could take Buck on his road tour.

Hammer agreed, so my father toured with him for a year, and Buck got to see a whole new world. Hammer and I were close, so he really did it as a favor to me. But Buck was just such a likable guy that people would fall in love with him, just meeting him. His personality was that strong.

During that year he was just there, kickin' it, and he made up his own job. He'd watch Hammer's back, and he didn't let nobody get too close to him. He was just having a good time, but that was his life. Coming up, he was a dancer, an entertainer, a player. Fast on his feet and he had been a good athlete when he was young. I think now that the Lord gave him that year to see some things, because he passed away shortly after the tour ended.

I'm convinced the Lord wanted Daddy Buck to see the world one time before his time was up. But his death was traumatic to me. It devastated me. He wasn't really there for me growing up, but we developed a relationship later on, and whatever else people may say about him, he was still my father.

My mother was the first in her family to come to Florida. She was born in Albany, Georgia, where she graduated from Madison High School in 1965. She came to Fort Myers to attend Edison College, and that's where she first met my father, at a get-acquainted dance her first week in town. Buck Sanders didn't waste any time. He was flashy, handsome, well dressed, and he just swept Connie up and they danced the night away.

They were married a year or so after that but they were already divorced by the time I turned three years old. Mother knew, probably from the very beginning, that Buck wasn't going to be a family man. She couldn't count on him, but they remained friends, even after she was remarried.

Daddy Buck was no more than 130 pounds soaking wet. He was about 5 feet 10, but he was bone thin. Before he passed away he really deteriorated. I remember going to see him. We didn't talk like father and son. We talked like homeys. I'd say, "What's up, Doc?" and he'd say, "Hey, baby boy, it's all good, baby." That's the way we talked. He'd hit me up for some cash, and he'd say, "I'm straight, baby, you know that. Let me hold a little something." And I'd say, "Look here, Daddy Buck, you don't need no money. Don't go asking me for no money now, you hear!"

But even when we were acting like brothers, like homeys, we never got close enough for him to say, "I love you," and that still haunts me to this day. I remember that I was playing baseball with the Braves when I got the phone call, "Deion, your father's dying. You need to come on home."

I came home, but by the time I got there he wasn't coherent, so I could only speak to him briefly on his deathbed. Just seeing him like that was devastating. We had really just started getting close. In some ways we had been close all my life, but now I was taking him places with me like my partner, and you talk about flamboyant! He would say, "You know I'm the reason for all this, don't you, baby! Wasn't for me there wouldn't be no Prime Time!"

He'd say, "I don't know but you better ax somebody, baby! The hands are still there but the legs are gone!" He'd slap some dap on me and say, "Shoot, baby, please! Look here, I mean, you know I got game!" And he did. I wish I had a tape of him. I'd love to hear him say it all one more time. But that was him. He was off the hook!

One of a Kind

Since my father's nickname was Daddy Buck, I started calling my own son Bucky, after him. Daddy Buck was really something. Never hurt nobody, loved everybody. But going to the funeral and seeing him like that was a traumatic experience for me. The first funeral I ever went to was my father's, and it was very tough.

Even after they were divorced, he and my mother remained good friends right up to the end. Even though they weren't together, they were still straight. He used to come by the crib and kick it with my folks, and he and my stepfather were tight.

My stepfather, whose name was Will Knight, used to take him in the car wherever he needed to go. Daddy Buck would come by and hit him up for a ride and he'd say, "Oh, thank the Lord for Will! Where there's no Will there's no way. You know I need you, Will!"

My stepfather was more like me. He was laid back, cool, relaxed. He had been in the house more years than anybody since I was seven or eight years old. He was a humble man but he drank too much. So far as I know he only drank at home. Never bothered anybody, never said anything. He'd just sit there, watch TV, and drink his beer. He would come home from work, go right into the house, have a few beers, and sit there listening to his gospel music until it was time to go to bed. Then he'd go right to bed and go to sleep.

Will Knight was never mean to me, never abusive, but that's how he was. He was the one that introduced me to fishing, and that's something I've always loved to do. But in both cases our roles were reversed. Those men were supposed to be my fathers, but in fact most of the time I wound up fathering them.

My stepfather would always tell me he came to my games but I never saw him there. Later he'd tell me everything about the game and he'd know all about it, so I figured he had to be there somewhere, but he was a shy man. He never wanted to be around people much, and I think he probably parked his truck off in the back somewhere and just watched quietly by himself.

I have some of that reserve in me too. Most people wouldn't believe it because when they see me on the field I'm flashy and outspoken, but the real Deion Sanders is naturally quiet and laid back. I don't really feel comfortable around a lot of people. I mean, if I had my wishes, I'd take my house and move it out in the middle of a hundred acres and sit out there and fish all day. That's what I'd love to do; but, unfortunately, I don't get to do that in my line of work.

As I said earlier, I invented the character of Prime Time in college, but I didn't have to look very far for my model. Daddy Buck was already there, and he was my biggest fan. Buck could just pop up out of nowhere. I remember one time at Florida State when we were playing the Miami Hurricanes at Doak Campbell Stadium in Tallahassee. I was getting ready to return a punt, and there were fifty or sixty thousand people up in the stands cheering and yelling, but I could hear this one voice clear as a bell, saying, "Baby boy, take it back! Take it back!" And I looked up into the stands and, sure enough, there he was sitting on the 50-yard line.

I don't know how he got a ticket or how he even got in, but he just went up there and shot game. He had so much of it! He shot game with somebody and they put him on the 50. I mean, we're talking about a man who could talk Muhammad Ali out of his boxing gloves! And he wasn't afraid to tell anybody who his son was. He'd say, "Oh, I'm here, baby boy! This is what you been lookin' for. Daddy Buck is here!"

My aunt Scoodie, who is Buck's younger sister, has been close to me for a long time, and she used to come up to Florida State with my father on weekends to see me play. She says that several times they would be sitting up in the stands and Daddy Buck would just be talking to me down on the field. Not yelling, just talking, but she said it was spooky the way I always seemed to know what he was saying.

One time when we were playing down in Miami, Scoodie and Daddy Buck were sitting on about the 50-yard line but high up in the stands. The score was tight, the clock was running down, and the game was really getting critical. At one point, Buck just said in a normal tone of voice, "Get down." And as soon as he said it, I bent down. Buck wasn't yelling at me or anything, it was like he was just talking to me in a normal voice.

He said, "They coming at you on a screen from the back side. Turn around now." Scoodie says that the minute he said it, I turned around. Then Buck said, "Look left and you got it." I turned around, looked to my left, and immediately made the interception. That play stopped the Hurricanes from scoring and we were able to hold the ball for the last few seconds and we won the game.

But Scoodie says she thought that was really eerie! She thought Buck was just talking out loud like he always did, but from that minute on she began to think we had some type of strange telepathy going on, and maybe we did. It's true that I always seemed to know when he was talking to me. I told her later, "Scoodie, I can hear Buck when he's telling me something." She would say, "Deion, trust me, out of all the people in the stands today you couldn't possibly hear what Buck was saying." But I believe I did. At least I seemed to have an extraordinary sense of what to do on the field.

I told her, "I don't care what's going on down here, Scoodie, I can hear my father. I can always hear what Buck is telling me."

Everything he told me turned out to be right on the money. Scoodie says it made her a little nervous, thinking we might be communicating like that. So she told Buck, "I don't know you, Buck Sanders! You're something else. Let me just move one seat farther away from you!" And I guess that would have seemed spooky to anybody. As soon as Daddy Buck would say something, it would happen. But I honestly believe that, for whatever reason and by whatever means, he was coaching me from the stands. Maybe it was just because I craved his input in my life so much.

Unless it's an away game, Scoodie still comes to all my games. When I played for the Falcons, she used to come to the stadium wearing all my jewelry. She was a miniature Prime Time! I remember that she used to wear this one little button that had a picture of me when I played Pee Wee football in Fort Myers. She would always wear that button for good luck, and before the game I would go by the stands and say, "Scoodie, you got your button?" And she'd say, "Yeah, Deion, I got my button. Everything's going to be all right." And it was.

I remember another time when I took Buck to a game with me in Miami. We had an open week at Florida State so I went down with a couple of my homeboys to see the Hurricanes play South Carolina. I had a lot of friends that played for Miami and we got tickets through them. But while we were driving down there I told Buck, "Now I ain't got but three tickets, Buck," and he said, "Don't worry about me, baby boy. I'm straight."

I wasn't sure he believed me, so I said, "I want you to hear me, Daddy Buck: I don't have a ticket for you. I ain't got but three tickets." But he just waved me off and said he was cool.

So we took him on down to the stadium and when we pulled up in front, I said, "Buck, you know just about everybody in Miami, so go on and have a good time and we'll check in with you after the game. Pick us up back here in three hours."

He took the car, but I could see he was really mad at me because we didn't have a ticket for him. But we went ahead into the game and found our seats, and they turned out to be really lousy seats. But no sooner had we sat down than one of the guys spotted Daddy Buck going down the aisle with a stocking cap on his head. I don't know where he got the cap, I don't know how he got in, but he just went on by us, walking right down to the 50-yard line, and as soon as he got to his seat he looked back at me and said something I can't repeat. And then he watched the rest of the game by himself!

I don't know what kind of game he shot or how he did it, but he was right down on the 50 and we were way back up there in the nosebleed section. I mean, he was off the hook! To this day he's still a legend in my hometown.

Even though they were separated, my mother always sort of looked out for Buck. She was like a second mother to him, and I guess it was a strange relationship. But it didn't seem strange to me at the time. Even though I grew up with my stepfather, she looked out for Daddy Buck, too, and my stepfather liked him because he knew Buck was a trip!

My biological father worked at a place called the Sunland Center, which was a home for mentally handicapped people in Fort Myers. He was the athletic director at this place. That was fine, but I remember that he would show up at every high school game with a busload of handicapped kids, and he always timed it perfectly. I don't know how he did it, but right when our bus was pulling up, or right when we'd be coming out of the locker room, we'd look up and there was Buck sitting in the stands with a hundred retarded folks.

My boys would just crack on me so hard! They would say, "Hey, Deion, there goes your daddy, man, with all those doctors and lawyers and stockbrokers!" They used to kill me about that! And Buck would just look at me and say, "Yeah, baby boy, I'm here!"

If that wasn't enough, he used to bet on the games! Even when I played Pee Wee football, Buck would come up to me and say, "Now look here, baby boy. I got a little something on this game, you see, so make sure you break those turkeys off today, you hear me?" I'm serious! I'd usually score four or five touchdowns anyway, so winning the game wasn't my biggest worry, but he was out there betting on the Pee Wee football game!

Sharing a Word

I had a chance to speak at both my fathers' funerals, to say how much they meant to me and how they had loved my mother and respected her. It was very hard for me. I couldn't keep from getting tears in my eyes right in the middle of my talk. My stepfather had all my rings. He had every ring I ever earned, including my state rings, World Series rings, Super Bowl rings. Everything I had. He really treasured those mementos.

Sometimes he would get all dressed up and put all those rings on his hands and just ride around like that, showing everybody how he felt about his boy. He was really proud of me and that's how he showed it. I've often said that he was the stepfather sent from God. A lot of stepfathers aren't there for you, or they're cold or abusive, but that wasn't the case with Willie Knight. He was a blessing in my life.

I'm constantly being invited to speak all around the country. I can't possibly accept all the speaking opportunities I'm offered, and I don't think that's where my focus needs to be right at this moment. I know there are things I can say, and in time I will have a lot more to say, but I think God wants me where I am for right now. So I just try to discern what the Lord is saying and I go where He leads me. I could travel and speak all the time if I didn't put some restraints on it, but for now I'm keeping my focus a little closer to home.

For example, I make regular visits to a local nursing home each week, and I teach a class at some of the high schools in Dallas where I live. In addition to football and baseball and all the professional engagements I have to keep, I visit with students at three schools in the Dallas area on a fairly regular basis. On Tuesday nights I act as moderator for "Prime Time Tuesdays" Bible study, which meets at a church in Plano, Texas. Most weeks, Pastor David Forbes flies down to teach the lesson for us, and that's a special time for me.

I consider my conversations with young people to be some of the most important work I do. When I teach in the schools, I deal with values, ethics, life strategies, the trials and tribulations of growing up in modern times, and all kinds of things like that. I talk about maturity, communication, discipline, love, fear, dealing with depression, and anything else that might help these kids get through all the junk that everybody's throwing at them all the time. There's a lot of anger out there, and a lot of kids feel they've been deserted by their families and by other adults. So I try to deal with that.

One of the schools where I teach is in a very upscale neighborhood, with a predominantly affluent white student body. Another school is in a more urban, less affluent, predominantly black and Hispanic area. I see both of these very different groups of students on a regular basis. The kids have a lot in common. Their fears, hopes, longings are a lot alike. But their attitudes regarding material things are very different.

By and large, the black kids I see are hurting because they feel they've been suppressed and held back. They haven't grown up with "things," and that's what they think they need. Television and the popular culture have told them they're supposed to have all that stuff, so they don't understand when they can't get it. They don't realize they have to earn it; they just think they're entitled to it.

But on the other side of the coin, a lot of the more affluent kids have things and they don't appreciate it. It's just a whole different atmosphere. Some of these young people are rebellious at home, fighting with their moms and dads. And all of them are getting a car for their sixteenth birthday and they don't realize that that's not how the rest of the world lives. So I tell them, "Okay, you crybabies! I'm going to take you over to some of the other parts of town and let you see the difference." And I say, "You guys ought to be thankful for what you've got."

Recently at one of the schools in north Dallas, we dealt with the concepts of responsibility and setting priorities. I went around the room and asked various students, "What are your responsibilities?" After we made the circuit, I came back around again and asked them, "Okay, now what are your priorities?" Those two things should be a lot alike, but in most cases I got totally different and sometimes contradictory answers between the first and second rounds.

So I asked them, "How can your responsibilities not be your priorities?" If you have a responsibility—whether it's schoolwork, homework, athletics, a part-time job, or whatever it is—that should be a priority for you. Too often they don't think about things like that, and kids these days don't make the connection between what they're expected to do and what they want to do. What I try to do is challenge young people to think about who they are, where they're going in life, and what sort of values they'll need to get there.

The schools usually give me as much time as I want, but these sessions usually run about forty-five minutes to an hour—about one regular class period. But there's a lot of time for interaction. We always go back over whatever we talked about the previous week. I ask them to recap where we've been. But then we take a little more each week and deal with some issues. I especially enjoy working with kids who have some influence in their group, whether it's good or bad, because I know these are the kids who can make a difference.

I like to reach kids who are leaders, who have strong moral values and a lot of ambition. But I also get some kids who have leadership skills and a lot of charisma, but they're using it in the wrong way. So this is an ideal mix for me, to get to talk to kids who influence other people, and then to lead them through some of the concepts and ideas that can make a real difference in their lives. I don't think there's any point in just talking to at-risk and problem children, because that usually develops into a therapy session or a contest of wills. The best situation is to get a roomful of young people who can really do something with what they learn and then just getting into it. I really enjoy doing that.

Everybody knows that gangs are a major issue in the schools these days. Some kids gravitate to gangs because they think they can get love, acceptance, protection, or a sense of identity there. I think they're really looking for the relationships they're not getting at home. But what they're actually finding is that the gang experience is a pretty sad compromise.

The gang is not really going to give them any of the things they want. A gang is a hard, cold, self-serving and exploitative relationship. People get hurt in gangs, and some of them end up crippled for life—not just physically, but emotionally—because of the lousy values and the false hopes associated with gang life. When they really get involved, they do stuff that either gets them in jail or dead, so I try to give them some other options.

They may think it's safe. But I tell them that when they get into a gang, the devil always takes them farther than they want to go and keeps them longer than they want to stay. He never shows them the full picture; he just shows them what he wants them to see. He gives them the sneak preview, the teaser. But he doesn't show them what will actually happen to their lives if they stay there very long. If they could only see what's ahead they would never even think about getting involved in that kind of stuff.

On the Other Side

Most of the time when I'm talking to people, I'm talking about love. High school kids are especially anxious to talk about love and relationships, but on the other side of the spectrum I also work with elderly people who have those same needs and emotions. When I go to the elderly home, I make it a point to visit with all the patients. Sometimes I sit down on their bedside and just talk to them. It may be no more than thirty seconds, but sometimes I stay for five or ten minutes and talk to them about how they're doing, what they're thinking about, or whatever else comes to mind.

It doesn't really matter whether they know me or not. Some of them are stuck in time and they don't recognize me from one week to the next. But that's okay. I visit them every week and sometimes it's like a soap opera. They all have different parts, different scenes to play, and different personalities. They're all at different places in their lives. They thank me for coming as if I was doing them a big favor, but you know, it's probably more of a blessing for me. They've seen so much, and I learn so much from them.

I know all of them now. I know that when I go in to see this one particular lady she's going to tell me that somebody's been stealing her money, because she says that every week. I know another lady is going to tell me all about her children, and another one will say she's feeling tired or feeling sick or she's worried that nobody loves her anymore. And there's one colorful old woman that's always going to scream at me and curse me out because she does it every week! But that's okay.

I think it's important to spend some time with those people each week. It prepares you for the changes in your own life. Some of those old people have wisdom. They've been through so much. And some of them just need a personal touch. Their children just take them there and leave them. But in some cases I suspect they're there because they were so bitter as parents that when they got old their kids just didn't want to put up with them anymore. And that should make all of us think about how we treat our own kids.

We're all going to be old someday. You're going to be old one day. What are they going to do with you? Are they going to leave you off at the elderly home because they don't want to deal with you? Are they going to put you away and forget you because you've always been so ugly and hateful and obnoxious? What are they going to do with you? I get so much by just being there, sitting on the bedside and visiting with these people. Unless someone from outside comes in to visit them and talk to them, a lot of them are not going to be loved or cared for, and they're not respected anymore. That has been very touching for me and a very eyeopening experience.

Life is a cycle, you know, and you end up like you started. When you were a baby, people had to take care of you, feed you, pick you up and put you in bed, change your diaper, and do all those things you couldn't do for yourself. And later, if you lose your mind or you're elderly and incapacitated or you don't know where you are, you may have to go back through that whole process all over again. It's a very odd cycle.

Now and then some of the patients get upset because the orderlies have moved them around. Or maybe the staff had to come in and clean the rooms or make the beds, and they did things that may have disturbed the old folks in some way—whether it's lifting them up, making them move around, or something else. But when I go in, I speak to them, touch them, and talk to them. Just being there is a ministry for me.

I do it because God put it on my heart. You know, it's funny what God does with me. He put it on my heart during baseball season in 1997 to work with the elderly. I was already working with high school kids before I became a Christian. I've always worked in the high schools wherever I'm playing. But God showed me that He wanted me to see the three different stages of life in one day.

Tuesday mornings I go to the high schools; Tuesday afternoon I go to the nursing home; and Tuesday evening I go to the Bible study. In that one day each week I see the three different age groups, and it's been such a blessing to me. Through my children, God has shown me the beginning of life. In my family and friends, I'm constantly exposed to the middle years of life and to the times of great accomplishment.

The toughest part has been learning to deal with the final stages of life. But seeing old age and death firsthand, as I have the last few years, has taught me a lot. It has helped me to reevaluate who I am and to reconsider my own goals and values. Coming close to death has helped me gain a new appreciation for life. Which sort of brings me back to where I started.

chapter eighteen

BEGINNING AGAIN

It's been very interesting for me to see the reactions of people to what they see happening in me. As long as I was in the world doing everything and anything to satisfy my lust and my pride, everything was cool. There were no restrictions and no limits to what I could say or what I could get involved in. But the minute I became a Christian, trying to steer clear of sin and controversy and anger, it was as if people felt they had to keep an eye on me to make sure I didn't do anything crazy! You would think they would want to jump on the bandwagon, but they were worried about what I might say.

But my walk with God has truly blessed my sports career, because now I'm able to put things in proper perspective. The Cowboys had a terrible season in 1997, but I felt it was a great season for me personally because, even though we lost ten games, we won spiritually. Because of the pressure and the turmoil we went through, a lot of players came to Christ that year. And as much as I hate losing and letting the fans down, when lives are changed like that you just have to see it as a victory. So in that regard, it was a great year.

Sometimes when an athlete has a conversion experience you'll see these little snide comments from the media. There's always the little suggestion, the innuendo, the hint that somehow you've gone around the bend. You've lost it, gone completely nuts and become a "born-again Christian." My career has remained about the same since I became a Christian, but I'm sure a lot of people will be watching to see what happens now. But that's cool. I hope they do, because they will see a new heart and a new sense of peace in my life.

I can remember sitting on the airplane on that long ride home after a losing game, hearing guys swearing and cursing about everything that went wrong. They reacted that way because they could only see that moment as the most important moment in their lives. I used to feel that way, too, but things are different for me now. When the last second ticks off the clock, that's it for me. The game is over.

Football is a game; it's not life! Of course I want to win every game I play and I'll give 110 percent every time I suit up; but in the end I want to know that I'm playing a game that has eternal ramifications. There's nothing that can be said or done on the football field that can discourage me anymore. If we lose on the football field, we lose. But that's not all there is to life.

Sometimes when we would fly in from a road game, I would sit there in my car at the airport praying for each of the guys on the team as they went home to their families. I would pray that they would all be able to go on with their lives, to put the disappointments behind them, and to have a sense of peace about this game. To this day my prayer is that every one of them will find the peace and joy that I've found.

There were lots of times when I would be talking to guys on the field, saying, "Hey, you guys are taking this thing way too seriously. It's just a game! You just have to do the best you can and let it go." Some of them would say, "Yeah, okay, Deion! That's easy for you to say, because you've got all that money. You're financially secure and you don't have to worry about anything else." But you know that's not the case at all.

Before I found Christ I had all the material comforts and all the money and all the fame and popularity, but I had no peace. When I found Christ, I found what I had been missing all those years. Only then was I able to trust in God's will for my life and, also, to relax and trust Him for the outcome. Sure, I always want to win. I always will. That's how I'm wired. The other players will tell you, nobody wants to win more than I do, and nobody works any harder to make it happen. But in the end, I have a new sense of peace about what happens both on and off the field.

I expect to have a long and successful career in football, but I've said this to the guys on the team: "You know, if the Lord told me to leave this game tomorrow, I could do that and never look back." Then I ask them, "Could you do that?" I've said to some of them, "Put aside the money, the celebrity, the cars and houses and all the opportunities this game has provided. Could you walk away from that?" I don't plan to leave football anytime soon, but I'm absolutely certain that when I do I will walk away from it without fear and without remorse if that's what the Lord wants me to do.

Knowing that has been a blessing for me. If you know where I've been and all the turmoil I went through before I got to this point, then you know what I'm talking about. People say stuff like, "This Christian stuff is going to ruin Deion's career. He's not going to be as aggressive anymore. He won't take chances like he used to. He won't even have the same edge to his game like he used to."

I mean, stupid articles were coming out for a while. But, you know what? It's just not true. I'm convinced that my walk with Christ has helped my game. If anything, I'm a better football player today than I was then, because now I'm playing for the Lord. I'm not just playing for Deion Sanders or Jerry Jones or the Dallas Cowboys. I'm playing for the Lord, to glorify Him. And the better I play, the more He's going to be glorified and the bigger the platform I'm going to have.

I don't know what it does for anybody else but I know I sure enjoy being with the Christian players from both teams when we get together on the field at the end of the game and kneel down and pray together. It's so good to put aside the rivalry and the competition and just to recognize that there is a bigger game going on in our lives than the one on the football field.

Other Avenues

People ask me, "Where is Deion going from here?" The answer is simple: ministry. God has called me to the ministry, and it's a high calling. It's no coincidence that Bishop Jakes is my spiritual father, my daddy in Christ. It's no coincidence that I met Pastor David Forbes the way I did. I was going to a charity basketball game and my agent wanted me to meet this guy who has a really dynamic ministry up in Columbus, and I agreed to do that. It's no coincidence that the Lord has surrounded me with all these wonderful people that have poured into my life.

A lot of people are confused about who Deion Sanders is and what's happened to me. They've seen the glory but they don't know the story. Some of them may not like me, but I go around giving my testimony so that at least they can understand what it is they don't like.

But I believe God has a high calling for me. Going around the country as I do on weekends during the off-season, I have seen people pour to the altar to receive Christ. God speaks to me in dreams and visions and He has showed me what He has in store for me. So I feel it's high calling. That's why He let me get to that point in the world, where I was, and He grabbed me from there. He gave me all the power, money, and fame, and then He grabbed me from that height and brought me onto His team.

Again, "For unto whomsoever much is given, of him shall be much required" (Luke 12:48 KJV). I've been blessed in very conspicuous ways, and I know that much will be required of me. A lot of people want to get in my shoes but they don't want to go through what I've been through to get here. It has taken a lot of bumps and bruises along the way, and a lot of bad decisions. But I've learned from all of them and I've been blessed.

When I think about all my achievements in the sports world, I realize just how very blessed I've been. I am still the only athlete to play in both the World Series and the Super Bowl. I was batting .533 at Atlanta in the 1992 Series, and I played for the 49ers during the 1994–95 season when we won Super Bowl XXIX and with Dallas in the 1995–96 season when we won Super Bowl XXX. I'm the only player in NFL history with both a pass reception and an interception return in Super Bowl action. I returned a 15-yard interception in Super Bowl XXIX, and I had a 47-yard reception in Super Bowl XXX, which turned out to be the longest pass completion of the game.

I'm the first two-way starter in the NFL since Chuck Bednarik played both sides for the Philadelphia Eagles back in the fifties and early sixties. I've had 34 career interceptions and 15 regular season touchdowns. In my first eight seasons as a runner, receiver, defender, punt returner, and kick-off returner, I gained an average of 17.7 yards every time I touched the football in a regular season game, and I have a career interception return average of 25.3 yards per return on 34 takeaways.

In baseball, I played for the New York Yankees in 1989–90, the Atlanta Braves from 1991 to 1994 while I was still at the Falcons in football, the Cincinnati Reds in 1994, 1995, and 1997, and then with the San Francisco Giants in 1995 when I was also playing for the 49ers in football. And of course I came back to the Cincinnati Reds and the Dallas Cowboys for the 1998–99 season.

That's wonderful stuff and I'm proud of all of it, but none of that success was enough to keep me from facing the reality of my situation and staring into the face of death. None of my success on the field could prepare me for the crisis in my life that led to my suicide attempt; nor could it prevent me from trying to end it all. I had chased too many phantoms and believed too many lies, and when I took that deadly plunge I had just reached the end of my rope.

On that fateful day in early 1997, I swerved off the road and when I slammed my foot down on the accelerator the car just shot up into the air like a rocket. But as it started to fall I sensed that something was wrong. By all rights, the car should have flipped or turned over or nosedived into the water, but that didn't happen, and things just didn't go like I thought they were going to. When I hit bottom, the car started sliding awkwardly, rocking back and forth, until I came down hard and slid to the bottom of the hill where the whole thing ended up in a pool of water.

Where was the big explosion? Where was the terrible crash? It didn't happen, and I just sat there with Kirk Franklin's music blasting away, and I laughed and shook my head. I couldn't even get that part right, and then I noticed the water starting to creep up into the car from the muddy stream bed where I had landed. I had gone over the cliff, all right, but it wasn't like I thought it would be.

Before long people were coming up, pounding on the windows of my car, and asking me if I was okay. But I wasn't even acknowledging that I knew they were there. Finally, after several minutes, somebody came down, pried open the door, and pulled me up out of the car. Then they helped me back up the hill and by this time police cars and ambulances started arriving, and one of the officers asked me, "What happened?"

I just looked him in the eye but I didn't say anything.

So he said, "Did somebody run you off the road?"

I shook my head and said, "No."

He said, "Did you lose control?"

Again, I looked him in the eye and said, "No." I might be crazy, but I wasn't a liar.

Finally the officer said, "Well, you have a choice, Mr. Sanders. You can either go down to the police station and file a report, or you can go with the ambulance and they'll check you out at the hospital and release you from there." So they agreed to call my attorney, and a little while later Eugene Parker came down to the hospital and picked me up. There wasn't a scratch on me.

After all that, Carolyn finally came up to Cincinnati and brought the kids, and she gave me all these lame excuses about why she hadn't come sooner. I didn't make it to the ballpark that night, and that was the first game I missed all season. After things got settled down, I had to go up to meet the team in Chicago, so we all flew down there together and I took my son and we had a great time. Carolyn came along, too, but she wasn't there emotionally.

By this time I was starting to make contact with various people who could see that I was in danger and they were reaching out to me. Bishop Jakes had actually prophesied eight months earlier that I would turn from my past and come to the Lord, but as I began to consider what was happening in my life, I began to discover that God was allowing Carolyn and me to grow farther apart for a reason. Through the struggles and the doubts and the bitterness, He was bringing me to the point where I could see His hand in my life.

Hunger and Thirst

Today I believe that if things had kept going as they were before all that happened, and if Carolyn and I had somehow found a way to patch things up and keep the family together, I probably would never have discovered who I really am. I would never have become a Christian, and I probably would not have survived the year: I'm convinced that God hardened Carolyn's heart against me so that she was unable to give me the kind of interaction I thought I needed at that time.

God wanted me to know that He was the Interactor I needed most in my life at that moment, and not some other person. But He had to get me to the point where He could do what He wanted to do with me, and that meant that first He had to strip me of all the comforts, all the success, and all the relationships that I had depended on.

We're not through with all of this yet, even today, but I can say this: If it wasn't for what Carolyn did, and if it wasn't for the way she responded during that difficult time, I wouldn't be where I am right now. I'd still be out there owning nightclubs, messing around with other women, hanging out with my homeys, and chasing after power, money, and sex.

I would still be believing that those things could solve all my problems. But if things hadn't started to get better in my spiritual life, I wouldn't be where I am. I'm a fast learner and I don't usually repeat my mistakes, so it's a pretty good bet I would have succeeded the next time I tried to end it all.

For the moment, I've lost the kind of access to my family that I'd like to have. Even though I see my children a lot, about every other weekend, and they spend the whole summer with me, it's certainly not what I'd like. But God knows what He's doing, and I know that all things work together for good for those who love Him (Rom. 8:28).

But I thank the Lord that He allowed the devil to come in and do those things, because if He hadn't, I wouldn't be where I am. And, in particular, I thank Carolyn for what she did, too. Because she got me to thinking, and even the court process and all the disputes back and forth helped me gain a new level of insight and a new perspective I desperately needed.

When I talk about these things today, I sometimes say it's a little like the book of Job in the Old Testament. God let down the hedges so the devil could come in and attack Job. God told the devil, "You can do everything but kill him. You can take his family; you can take his fortune; but you can't have his life." I thank the Lord that He chose to spare me and give me a new start.

Up to that point in my life I always assumed that most Christians were hypocrites. I knew some hypocrites when I was growing up and I didn't want to be like that. I've always been the kind of person that, if I talk it, I'm going to walk it. And if I'm gonna say it, then I'm going to display it. That's the way I am. So I avoided getting involved with Christianity because I was confused about what the Christian is all about.

But confusion is not of God, and I wasn't seeing the real thing. I was under the illusion that if I ever wanted to be a Christian I had to get my life straightened out first. It was like taking a brand-new car to the car wash, or taking a brand-new suit to the cleaners. I thought I had to do my own thing so I would be good enough for God to save. But what I eventually discovered was that you don't get yourself together to come to Christ. You come to Christ so you can get yourself together.

Bishop Jakes, who came into my life through all of that stuff, is so real, so honest, so bold, and he is one of the most compassionate people I've ever met. He's a man of integrity, of high morals and high standards. I see him as a man who knows God, and for him to have become not only my spiritual father but my mentor and friend has been a blessing I can't even begin to describe.

As a man who is consciously and expectantly growing in the grace and knowledge of Jesus, I want to be filled with the Word, and the ministry of the Word is so important to me now. Bishop Jakes has helped focus me and direct my eyes so that I can see what the Bible says and what it means for my life.

Bishop has filled my well in ways he doesn't even know. I have no doubt that the Lord placed him in my life at the precise moment when it would mean the most to me. With the passing of my father and stepfather within just a short time of each other, I was really devastated; so being able now to have an ongoing personal relationship with such a mighty man of God has been a tremendous blessing for me. He's not just a spiritual father to me, but he's a father, a mentor, and a dear friend.

He has the type of character and personality that I can model myself on. It's really ironic that Bishop Jakes should become my spiritual father, because there are so many similarities, personally, emotionally, businesswise, and even the way we think. It's scary sometimes. I remember one time when I was in the bathtub and Bishop was on my heart, and just at that moment the phone rang and it was him, calling to see if I was doing all right.

I remember driving back from Houston on another occasion and I was feeling very troubled in my spirit; I had just had a big argument with my ex-wife, and the phone rang in the car and it was Bishop Jakes, out of nowhere, just calling to see how I was doing. It's amazing, but he is so tuned in to the Holy Spirit that he seems to know when I'm hurting and he's there to minister to me. Of all the men I've known in my life, he's the only one I've been able to call Daddy.

I know it's not unusual to see people get excited about the Christian life and then they fall off after a while. And it's not unusual to see people just drag along for a period of time until finally they get tired of doing the hokey-pokey and they just jump off the fence and go ahead and do what they have to do. When I caught on fire, it was for the long run. Since I was delivered I have stayed on fire and just increased that passion to learn more.

I give a lot of the credit for my growth to the people God has surrounded me with. Birds of a feather flock together. Or as Pastor David Forbes would say, association breeds assimilation. The people God has brought into my life are people who are all flying at a pretty high level. In order to fly with them, I have had to pull back on the yoke and rudder and learn to soar at a whole new altitude of faith and spiritual discernment.

The teachers and ministers who have come into my life are feeding me so much right now, but I realize that at some point my own voice and ministry will begin to emerge. For the time being I'm doing my best to learn from the best of all the various influences I'm being exposed to. And perhaps one day evangelist Deion Sanders will be ready to use a combination of the gifts, abilities, and talents that God has provided so that I can share my testimony, preach the gospel, and share with others what I have learned in a way that may pierce the heart.

I try to be on my guard at all times against the wiles of the devil because he knows me and he knows where all my doors and windows are. But I've taken away the welcome mat and Jesus is standing guard at the doors to my heart. I have a passionate hunger for the things of God, and each day I'm feeding on His Word. Jesus said, "Blessed are those who hunger and thirst for righteousness, for they shall be filled" (Matt. 5:6), and that's how I want to be. I want more of what God has to offer, and He has graciously allowed me to have access to some mighty men of faith who make sure that I'm constantly filled with the Word.

Fame and fortune have given me a unique perspective on life. I had everything that power, money, and sex could give me but it just wasn't enough. I had the biggest, the best, the fastest, the baddest, and the meanest stuff anybody could want and it didn't satisfy me. I realized that I was empty inside. Desperately empty.

Some people might say, "Yeah, I need the Lord, but I need money, too." Whereas, because of my wealth and position, I had to face the fact that power, money, and sex had not satisfied me or solved my problems. So I had to admit, "Well, I've got all the money anybody could want and

I'm still empty. So whatever I'm missing, it's not that!" People with a lot of money can insulate themselves from pain with their comfortable lifestyles for a while, and some of them manage to stay so isolated and so numbed that they never have to acknowledge the hurt they feel deep down inside.

But now and then God allows a certain level of pain to work its way through, and today I believe that the power and the privileges I enjoyed as a professional athlete only made certain that sooner or later I would come to the point where either success would destroy me or I would have to see that only God could save me.

Success almost ruined my life, but, thank God, I came to Him just in the nick of time. And that has made all the difference.

Royalty proceeds generated from the sale of this
book are being donated to the Potter's House in Dallas, Texas.